PLUMAS NATIONAL

Trout Fishing
Guide

ANDREW HARRIS

Frank Amato

PORTLAND

PLUMAS NATIONAL FOREST
Trout Fishing
Guide

ANDREW HARRIS

Frank Amato PORTLAND

DEDICATION

To my mother, Marny, and my father, John, who gave me the motivation to pursue my dreams.

ACKNOWLEDGMENTS

My sincere gratitude is extended to my family for their thoughtful comments and criticisms. I would especially like to thank my sister, Karen, who joined me on several photographic expeditions, and my mother, Marny, who collected vast quantities of historical information from the Plumas County Museum. Without their help this book would not be complete. I would also like to thank Milt Jensen (Merganser Outfitters), Allan Bruzza at the Sportsman's Den in Quincy, Dave Takahashi at the Grizzly Country Store on Lake Davis, Ron Decoto at the California Department of Fish and Game, and the helpful people at the United States Forest Service.

Published in 1999 by:
Frank Amato Publications, Inc.
PO Box 82112 • Portland, Oregon 97282 • (503) 653-8108

Softbound UPC: 0-66066-00375-1
Softbound ISBN: 1-57188-175-1

All photographs taken by the author unless otherwise noted.
Cover Photo: Karen Harris Boone

Book Design: Tony Amato

Printed in Canada

10   9   8   7   6   5   4   3   2   1

Contents

PLUMAS
National
Forest

Introduction

Somewhere between Hat Creek and Yosemite, between the McCloud River and Mammoth Lakes, lies one of the greatest undiscovered fly-fishing areas in California. Covering over one million acres, the Plumas National Forest is home to three branches of the Feather River, hundreds of small streams, dozens of lakes, and four species of trout. Just an hour and a half from Reno, three hours from Sacramento, and four to five hours from the Bay Area, the Plumas National Forest is a great place to get away from it all and enjoy some fine trout fishing set against a backdrop of beautiful scenery.

Fly-fishers new to this area will be pleasantly surprised to find light fishing pressure on most of the waters. Even the best roadside waters are seldom crowded, and a half-hour hike to a small lake or stream will guarantee complete isolation. First-time visitors will also be amazed with the great variety of fly-fishing opportunities in the Plumas National Forest. There are rough boulder-strewn rivers, expansive reservoirs, spring creeks, backcountry lakes, and multitudes of small streams.

My objective in authoring this book is to provide the angler with the knowledge to tackle the lakes and streams of the Plumas National Forest with confidence. It is my intention that this book also be of value not only to those who fish, but to hikers, tourists, backpackers, hunters, picnickers, and those who faithfully accompany fly-fishers on their journeys.

OREGON

NEVADA

• REDDING

PLUMAS
NATIONAL
FOREST

• RENO

• SACRAMENTO

• SAN FRANCISCO

CALIFORNIA

PACIFIC
OCEAN

Part One..

THE PLUMAS NATIONAL FOREST: PAST, PRESENT, AND FUTURE

Looking at the Forest Service map of the Plumas National Forest, one can see that it covers an incredibly vast amount of land. Its one-million-plus acres encompass parts of Plumas, Butte, Sierra, and Yuba counties, well over 1% of the state of California. The Forest Service estimates that there are nearly 100 million trees in the Plumas National Forest. To put that number in perspective, the area surrounding the National Forest is home to less than 25,000 people.

The Plumas National Forest is a very scenic area. Encompassed within the boundaries of the forest are breathtaking waterfalls, sheer granite cliffs, vast stands of timber, and rugged canyons. You can get an inkling of this beauty by driving along Highway 70, the main thoroughfare through the region. Highway 70 winds through the Feather River Canyon alongside the North Fork of the Feather River. In some places the rim of the canyon is nearly a vertical mile above the river. In the streambed you will notice a jumble of enormous boulders, all worn smooth by the force of water. Small waterfalls cascade down the side of the canyon.

The roadside scenery is just the beginning. To see more of the majesty of the area, venture off on sideroads and trails. The Middle Fork of the Feather River is very beautiful in its sheer ruggedness. Some of the trails into the Middle Fork end several hundred vertical feet above the river in sections reminiscent of the Grand Canyon. The small canyons of the tributary streams offer countless delights, from rocks covered with ladybugs to impassable waterfalls. Evidence of ancient and recent human activities provide endless intrigue. Indian rocks, depressions worn in granite by the process of grinding nuts and grain, dot the landscape. Remains of mining camps and equipment dating back to the 1850s are plentiful.

Before you can truly appreciate the majesty of this or any other area, you must force yourself to slow down and absorb your surroundings. All too often I find myself focusing so intently on the fishing that I don't see anything other than the water. The American wilderness is a beautiful thing, and many of us choose the sport of fly fishing as our way to partake of this treasure. However, we mustn't let ourselves become so involved in our fishing endeavors that we forget to look at the scenery that surrounds us.

Accessing the Plumas National Forest

The Plumas National Forest can be accessed from the Lake Almanor area to the north via Highway 89. Highway 70 offers access from the Sacramento Valley on the west and Reno to the east. The Plumas National Forest can be accessed via Highway 89 from the Tahoe area to the south. The Oro-Quincy Highway is a good paved route from Oroville to the Bucks Lake and Quincy area.

A Guided Tour Following the Pacific Crest Trail

Over seventy-five miles of the Pacific Crest Trail wind through the Plumas National Forest. The Plumas is just one of twenty-four national forests crossed by the Pacific Crest Trail on its 2,500-mile journey from Canada to Mexico. There is an incredible variety of wildlife, terrain, water, and trout encompassed within the boundaries of the Plumas National Forest. A short tour along the Pacific Crest National Scenic Trail is a good way to give you an idea of this variety.

Blazing its way south from Mount Lassen and the Lassen National Forest, the Pacific Crest Trail enters the Plumas National Forest on its northwestern boundary near Belden. Following Chips Creek, the trail descends into the Feather River Canyon, famous for its scenery, both natural and architectural. The North Fork of the Feather River winds its way through this canyon from Lake Almanor towards the expansive Lake Oroville. In the headwaters of the North Fork are Yellow Creek, Indian Creek, and Butt Valley Reservoir, some of the finest waters in the national forest.

From Belden, the Pacific Crest Trail climbs 4,00[
Lakes and the Bucks Lake Wilderness. There are numer
take in this recently created wilderness, including hikes
Lost Lake, down the Mill Creek or Right Hand Branch ...
to Bucks Lake, or down the Granite Gap Trail to Gold Lake and Silver
Lake. The Pacific Crest Trail continues southward towards Lookout
Rock, at 5,964 feet, then drops almost 3,000 feet into the Wild and Scenic
canyon of the Middle Fork Feather River.

The Pacific Crest Trail crosses high over the Middle Fork on a
beautiful single-arch footbridge. There are dozens of other trails that
reach the Middle Fork Feather River, but the Pacific Crest Trail is the best
maintained and has the lowest gradient. There are many good campsites
where the trail crosses the river. In the headwaters of the Middle Fork
Feather River are lakes Davis and Frenchman, two of the best trout
reservoirs in the state of California. Climbing up out of the Wild and
Scenic canyon, the Pacific Crest Trail crosses the headwaters of the South
Fork Feather River near Little Grass Valley Reservoir.

The last stop on the Pacific Crest Trail before it leaves the
Plumas National Forest is the Lakes Basin, a popular destination for
family vacations. There are dozens of trails in the Lakes Basin (not to be
confused with the Sixty Lakes Basin in the Sequoia-Kings Canyon
National Park), including the Jamison Lake Trail, Long Lake Trail, and
Bear Lakes Loop. Each of these trails interconnects with the others and
with the Pacific Crest Trail. Some of the lakes most easily reached from
the Pacific Crest Trail include Deer Lake, Round Lake, Wades Lake, and
Gold Lake. Traveling southward from the Lakes Basin, the Pacific Crest
Trail parts with the Plumas National Forest, heading south on its long
journey to Mexico.

History of the Plumas National Forest

During my explorations of the Plumas National Forest, I am frequently
reminded of a passage in *Illustrated History of Plumas, Lassen & Sierra
Counties* (Farris & Smith: San Francisco, CA. 1882.). "Every bar, bend,
hill, flat, and ravine is replete with stirring scenes and interesting events

he pioneer of thirty years who again revisits the scene of his early adventures; while to the man of to-day they present but the ordinary features of nature." That passage was written in 1882, and by that time nature had already erased much of the evidence of the human meddling that took place only three decades earlier. The forces of nature have now had almost 150 years to erase the evidence of the California Gold Rush and its early consequences. In most areas nature has succeeded, and it is only through the vigilance of historians that thousands of artifacts and priceless stories of old have been preserved.

To gain a complete understanding of the history of the Plumas National Forest, one must begin before the Gold Rush with the naming of the Feather River, or Rio de Las Plumas, from which Plumas County and the Plumas National Forest take their names. The first historical account of the Feather River is in the 1833-34 diary of a fur trapper by the name of John Work, although many early histories of the area claim that Captain Luis A. Arguello named the river in 1820 during a Spanish exploration of the Sacramento Valley. Many theories exist as to the reason for the name, but the predominant theory is that the river was named after the feathers used by the local Valley Maidu Indians.

The Valley and Mountain Maidu were the only people to inhabit the Feather River area prior to the Gold Rush. Despite the discovery of gold in California in January 1848, the ruggedness of the headwaters of the Feather River discouraged visitors until the spring of 1850. The first major exploration of the area occurred when Thomas Robertson Stoddart led a group of men in search of a mythical lake with shores of gold. The lake was never found, and Stoddart (by then referred to as Crazy Stoddart) narrowly escaped being hanged by his disappointed crew.

Although the lake with shores of gold was never found, the "Gold Lakers" went on to make some of the biggest gold strikes in California, such as Rich Bar and Nelson Point. Panning and sluice-boxing were the most common mining methods in the early years when the gold was thick in the streams. As the streams were worked over and gold became more scarce, miners turned to hard-rock mining and hydraulic mining. Quartz veins were tapped by impressive networks of tunnels. Entire mountainsides were washed away by the hydraulic miners. Both methods required the construction of flumes to harness the energy of falling water. The hard-rock miners used water to drive ore-crushing stamp mills. Hydraulic miners built flumes to channel water into nozzles, or monitors, that were aimed at gold-bearing hillsides. The flumes built to carry all this water are still in evidence throughout the Plumas National Forest.

As mining became less productive during the late 1800s, the people of Plumas County began to look for new ways to make a living. Many who didn't find wealth in gold found a living in farming the lush valleys of the area, and these men went on to become the founding fathers of Plumas County and the towns that lie therein. Still others began to turn their attention to the vast stands of timber that adorned the landscape. Thousands of distraught miners found a new livelihood in the logging industry. The realization of the area's logging potential eventually led to the establishment of the Plumas National Forest.

In 1905 President Theodore Roosevelt established the Plumas, Diamond Mountain, and Lassen forest reserves (national forests were called forest reserves in those days). All three reserves, a combined area of over three million acres, were entrusted to Supervisor Louis A. Barrett, who temporarily set up shop in a Quincy saloon. Common duties for Barrett and his staff included investigating bogus mining claims, running down timber trespassers, and seeing who was grazing stock in the reserve. All three reserves were supervised by Mr. Barrett and a small staff until 1908, when a separate administration was created for the Lassen Reserve. The Forest Service has grown along with the creation of new recreational opportunities and increasing timber operations in the Plumas National Forest. The Plumas is now served by a large Supervisor's Headquarters in Quincy and six separate ranger stations.

As Barrett and his rangers chased down timber trespassers and poachers, an exciting development opened up new economic opportunities for Plumas County. The Western Pacific Railroad through the canyon of the North Fork Feather River was completed in 1909. For the first time, developers were able to feast their eyes on the riches of the Feather River Canyon. What they saw was not gold, but "white gold:" hydroelectric power. Although the first hydroelectric plant on the North Fork had been completed at Big Bend in 1908, the Great Western Power Company set plans in motion to build several new projects. Among the initial projects were the Bucks Creek Powerhouse (1928) and Caribou Powerhouse (1922). The Great Western Power Company was bought by Pacific Gas & Electric in 1930. PG&E continued to develop the river, building a series of power dams and powerhouses dubbed the "Feather River Canyon Stairway of Power." The North Fork of the Feather River now has the most installed hydroelectric capacity of any river in California.

As hydroelectric projects were under construction in the Feather River Canyon, the railroad was bringing growing numbers of tourists to the area. The first fish stockings took place in 1911, when over 300,000 fingerlings—a mixed bag of rainbow, eastern brook, and Loch Leven (brown trout)—were distributed amongst the lakes and streams of Plumas County. With this enormous planting the fishery of the Plumas National Forest was forever changed, arguably for the better. The Western Pacific Railroad inaugurated a "Fisherman's Special" that passed through the area on its round trip from Oakland to Salt Lake City. As the popularity of the Fisherman's Special increased, numerous resorts popped up along the rail line, including Tobin, Camp Rogers, Belden, Virgilia, Indian Falls, Paxton, and Keddie. In addition to wild and stocked trout, there were also steelhead and salmon in the forks of the Feather River in those days. The Feather River Canyon peaked as a fisherman's destination in the twenties and thirties.

The forties would see the end of the salmon and steelhead as the power dams were constructed. Cresta, Rock Creek, and Poe power dams were completed in 1949, 1950, and 1958, respectively, sealing off the North Fork of the Feather River. Lake Oroville dam was completed in 1967, blocking off the entire river system just above the city of Oroville. The Feather River Fish Hatchery below Oroville Dam was constructed to compensate for the reduction in spawning area. Lake Davis, Frenchman Lake, and Antelope Lake were also constructed during the sixties as a component of the California State Water Project.

Trout of the Plumas National Forest

The Plumas National Forest currently contains quite species, but that has not always been the case. Up unti only variety of trout to call this region home was the coastal rainbow steelhead trout. These native rainbows inhabited the major rivers and streams up as high as the first insurmountable block to their migration. All lakes, unless connected to the river systems by a decent outlet stream, were barren of trout. The small backcountry lakes we currently enjoy fishing were most likely fishless before man introduced trout to them. Other native fish include sculpins, Sacramento suckers, squawfish, hardheads, coho (silver) salmon, and chinook (king) salmon.

Rainbow Trout (*Oncorhynchus mykiss*)

The rainbow has the honorable distinction of being the only trout native to the Plumas National Forest. When the forty-niners swept through the region in search of gold, there existed two subpopulations of these native rainbows, sea-run steelhead and a resident population. Both subpopulations were of the coastal rainbow variety.

The sea-run fish were much larger, and often migrated well past the 3000-foot elevation level to spawn. Those steelhead were accompanied by even larger fish in those days, king and silver salmon. The silver salmon is no longer found in the Feather River drainage, and the remaining king salmon and steelhead can only run up as far as Oroville Dam, which was completed in 1967. Before the North Fork hydropower dams and the Oroville Dam, these magnificent fish were known to migrate as far up as Indian and Spanish creeks, in the headwaters of the North Fork Feather River.

Rainbow trout can now be found in almost every body of water . the Plumas National Forest. The main exceptions are small lakes that have no inlet streams suitable for spawning, and silty streams that are more suited to brown trout. The rainbows of the Plumas National Forest range in size from 10-pound lake-bound monsters to the minuscule inhabitants of the smallest creeks. The larger rainbows can be found in Lake Davis, Frenchman Lake, Butt Valley Reservoir, and the Middle and North Forks of the Feather River.

Since the advent of fish hatcheries and aggressive fish-stocking programs, many non-native rainbows have been introduced into the lakes and streams of the Plumas National Forest. The Department of Fish and Game currently stocks several domesticated varieties of rainbow trout, including Kamloops, Eagle Lake trout, and Coleman rainbows. Eagle Lake trout fingerlings are periodically stocked in Frenchman Lake and Lake Davis, among other places. These fingerlings grow very fast in these food-rich environments and provide excellent angling opportunities.

Brown Trout (*Salmo trutta*)

The first brown trout were most likely introduced to the Plumas National Forest about the time of its creation in 1905. These fish have become established in most of the streams in the area, although they are not caught as often as other species due to their wariness. Streams featuring high numbers of brown trout include Indian Creek, Grizzly Creek, and Yellow Creek. Browns can also be found in most lakes that have inlet streams suitable for spawning. Very large browns can be caught in the bigger impoundments, although catches are few and far between during the summer months.

They are available to anglers mostly in the spring and fall, and most are fooled by large streamer patterns. Several very large browns are also taken from the Middle and North Fork of the Feather River each season. These extremely wary fish usually fall victim to natural baits, but fly-fishers can effectively stalk these larger trout with big streamers and nymphs.

Brook Trout *(Salvelinus fontinalis)*

The brook trout, not requiring tributary streams to spawn, has been a blessing for many of our high-country lakes. Without these beautiful, sometimes overly prolific fish, hundreds of lakes throughout the Sierra Nevada would be unable to support wild populations of trout. Brookies were introduced to the Southern Sierras in the 1870s, but didn't make it as far north as the Plumas National Forest until the turn of the century or shortly thereafter. They now inhabit most of the lakes of the Lakes Basin, as well as numerous other small lakes throughout the national forest. They can also be found in most streams connecting lakes that support brook trout populations. Although the average brook trout is pan-sized, brookies up to three pounds can be found in several lakes in the Plumas National Forest. Three Lakes, Silver Lake, Taylor Lake, and several lakes in the Lakes Basin are well known for producing large brook trout. Hatchery operators have also taken a liking to these fish, and catchable brookies are now stocked in many of our lakes. Catchable brookies are stocked more or less annually at Gold Lake and Bucks Lake, and are often substituted for catchable rainbows in other waters when necessary.

Since brook trout have a propensity for overpopulation in most of our lakes and streams, the California Fish and Game Commission has adopted a Brook Trout Bonus Bag Limit that applies throughout the Plumas National Forest and most of the Sierra Nevada. You may keep ten brook trout less than eight inches long in addition to your normal five-fish limit. If you're fishing a small lake or stream that is overpopulated with stunted brookies, please take advantage of this bonus bag limit and keep fifteen fish. Pan-fried brook trout are a backpacker's delight.

Mackinaw (*Salvelinus namaycush*)

Mackinaw, or lake trout, have been introduced into two lakes in the Plumas National Forest, Bucks Lake and Gold Lake. Like brook trout, mackinaw are a type of char, not a true trout. Mackinaw are deep-water fish, requiring less oxygen than other trout. They prefer temperatures around 50 degrees, and are highly piscivorous. They were introduced in Bucks Lake in 1984 to curb the stunted kokanee population. I believe this attempt at biological control is working, although slowly. The kokanee have gotten a bit bigger, and I've never caught a mackinaw that didn't have a little kokanee in its stomach. Mackinaw were introduced into Gold Lake much earlier, in 1966. They were stocked again in 1979 and 1985, and the mackinaw fishery steadily improved. Fingerling lake trout are now stocked in Bucks Lake and Gold Lake on an annual basis.

Mackinaw grow to very large sizes in Gold Lake and Bucks Lake. The Bucks Lake record is a monster 30 pounder. Gold Lake macks are not far behind. Macks are most easily caught in the spring, when they are close to the surface. If one were absolutely hell-bent on catching a mackinaw on a fly-rod, I suppose a big leech or minnow pattern trolled slowly on a full-sink line behind a boat or float tube would be the best bet. I prefer to spend my time chasing rainbows and browns this time of year, and leave the mackinaw to the heavy-metal (downriggers and lead-core line) fishermen.

Kokanee *(Oncorhynchus nerka)*

Kokanee are a landlocked, dwarf form of the sockeye salmon. These silver-sided fish have been introduced into Bucks Lake and Little Grass Valley Reservoir, and some have washed out of Bucks Lake to inhabit Lower Bucks Lake as well. Kokanee subsist primarily upon zooplankton so they are a difficult target for the fly-fisher. However, kokanee may be taken on brightly colored flies, especially in the spring and fall when these fish are active on the surface.

Kokanee live for four years, attaining a length of ten to twelve inches in Bucks Lake and twelve to fourteen inches in Little Grass Valley Reservoir. In the fall of their fourth year the fish begin to change color, from a shiny silver to a dark red body with a greenish head. The males develop hooked jaws. During or after this metamorphosis, the kokanee begin their spawning run, ascending tributary streams in late September and remaining until November. The kokanee spawning run is very impressive at Bucks Lake, where the fish run up Bucks Creek. Thousands of fish cram this tiny stream every fall, competing for mates and space. The spawning grounds are so productive in Bucks Creek that the kokanee have become overpopulated in Bucks Lake. To combat this overpopulation, the California Department of Fish and Game collects the eggs from Bucks Creek to distribute to other lakes that lack sufficient natural reproduction, such as Little Grass Valley Reservoir. In the fall of 1996 over 1.5 million kokanee eggs were collected from Bucks Creek.

Other Fish

Trout aren't the only fish that can be found in the waters of the Plumas National Forest. Squawfish, Sacramento suckers, sculpins, and hard-heads are common in the forks of the Feather River. While you aren't likely to catch a sucker, you may often see them combing the bottom with their vacuum-cleaner mouths. The Sacramento sucker is actually a very pretty fish, having a brilliant orange belly. Riffle sculpins are also common, providing forage for the larger rainbows and browns. Sculpin imitations such as Whitlock's Sculpin and the Muddler Minnow will catch the attention of large trout when fished properly.

Hardheads and squawfish are members of the minnow family. Juvenile hardheads can be a nuisance in some streams as they are eager to take dry and wet flies. Squawfish are the largest of the non-trout species, and they mainly inhabit the lower regions of the North and Middle Fork Feather River. In the Middle Fork I have seen squawfish that were nearly three feet long. Squawfish will take nymphs, and often chase hooked trout that are being played. Oftentimes one can see enormous squawfish swimming lazily in the slow pools of the larger streams. An angler who can't tell the difference between a squawfish and a trout can get very excited upon seeing these large fish. You can tell the difference between them from a distance by their tails. Squawfish have deeply forked tails that are slightly transparent, while trout have more or less square, opaque tails. If you're catching squawfish instead of trout you're probably fishing in water that is too slow—try moving to a faster, more oxygenated part of the river.

Conservation, Catch & Release, and CalTrout

The sport of fly fishing is currently more popular than it has ever been in the United States. In many ways, the popularity of the sport is a good thing. Fly tiers are delighted with all the new materials on the market. The variety of high-quality rods, reels, and waders is ever increasing. The literature of the sport is growing to satisfy the ravenous curiosity of a growing audience. The bad news about the growing popularity of the sport is that a more-or-less finite resource is being shared between more and more people.

That resource is, of course, the trout. Put more accurately, the resource is the trout habitat. Whether the trout are allowed to utilize that habitat to the best of their natural ability is up to us. Pardon me for being so blunt, but a dead trout has a lot of trouble utilizing trout habitat. We can spend millions of dollars restoring and improving trout habitat, but the quality of the fishery still depends on the angler. If every fish over ten inches is kept, few fish will reach good size. If you must keep fish, please do so selectively. Limit your catch to hatchery fish, or find a small stream full of stunted brook trout and take advantage of the brook trout Bonus Bag Limit. These small fish taste better and fit more easily in the frying pan.

Conservation is especially critical in the state of California, the most populous state in the nation. California Trout, commonly referred to as CalTrout, was formed by a group of individuals concerned about the issues I have discussed. CalTrout has been around in one form or another since 1965. I can think of no better way to explain CalTrout than to quote its mission statement: "California Trout . . . is dedicated to protecting and restoring wild trout, native steelhead and the waters they inhabit throughout California; and to creating high quality angling opportunities for the public to enjoy." CalTrout volunteers have accomplished this goal at Yellow Creek and countless other waters throughout California.

One of the most essential components of fisheries conservation is the practice of releasing some or all of your fish so that they may grow and be caught again. I must emphasize that catch and release will do no good at all if practiced improperly. An angler that maims and releases ten fish will do much more damage than an angler that keeps five fish and releases none. Do not squeeze fish; cradle them gently. Wet your hands before touching the fish. Keep the fish in the water if at all possible. I've seen too many novices pull a fish up onto a sand bar, yank the hook out and throw the fish back in the water. Fish treated in this manner will die. Learn how to practice catch and release properly. The challenge of fishing is to catch the fish, not kill the fish.

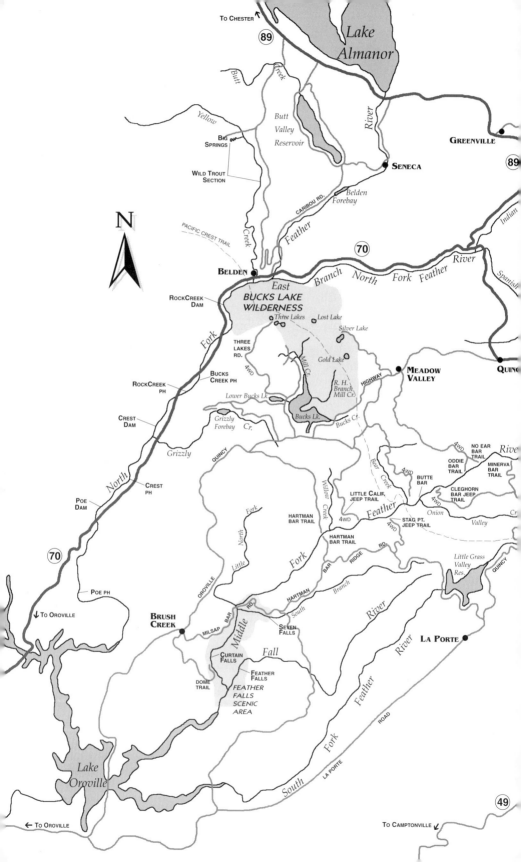

TO WESTWOOD ↑

Antelope Lake

Creek

Creek

Creek

Indian

PLUMAS NATIONAL FOREST

LEGEND

```
0   1   2   3   4   5
        MILES
```

━━━━ State Highways
─── Paved or gravel roads
- - - Trails
+ + + Railroad

Base map U.S. Department of Agriculture Forest Service

To purchase a Forest Service map of the Plumas National Forest, visit one of the Ranger District offices listed in Appendix B.

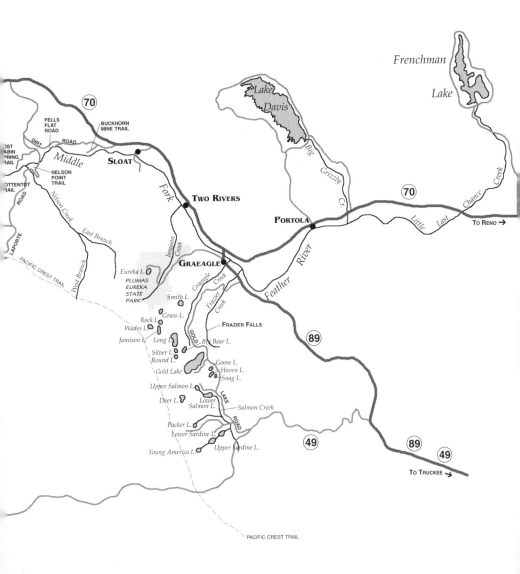

Frenchman *Lake*

70

FELLS FLAT ROAD

BUCKHORN MINE TRAIL

DIRT ROAD

OST ABIN PRING RAIL

Middle **SLOAT**

NELSON POINT TRAIL

OTTENTOT RAIL

Lake *Davis*

ROAD

LAPORTE

Fork

TWO RIVERS

Big Grizzly Cr.

70

Last Chance Creek

Little

TO RENO →

PACIFIC CREST TRAIL

Nelson Creek

East Branch

West Branch

Jamison Creek

Eureka L.

PLUMAS EUREKA STATE PARK

GRAEAGLE

PORTOLA

Feather *River*

Graeagle Creek

Frazier Creek

Smith L.

Grass L.

Rock L.
Wädes L.

Jamison L. Long L.

Silver L.
Round L.

Gold Lake

Upper Salmon L.

Deer L.

Lower Salmon L.

Packer L.
Lower Sardine L.

Young America L.

Upper Sardine L.

FRAZIER FALLS

GOLD

Big Bear L.

Goose L.
Haven L.
Snag L.

LAKE ROAD

Salmon Creek

89

49

89

49

TO TRUCKEE →

PACIFIC CREST TRAIL

Part Two..

LAKES AND STREAMS OF THE PLUMAS NATIONAL FOREST

I have divided the lakes and streams of the Plumas National Forest into six sections. Keep in mind as you read through the remainder of the book that I chose these sections mainly according to geographic convenience. One section is devoted to each of the forks of the Feather River. Two of the remaining sections, the Bucks Lake Area and Lakes Basin Area, describe distinct geographical areas. The last section, the Upper Feather River Lakes, conveniently groups Lake Davis, Frenchman Lake, and Antelope Lake together.

North Fork of the Feather River

The North Fork of the Feather River was once one of the finest trout streams in California, and may reclaim that status sometime in the future. Meanwhile, the river serves as a textbook example of the effects of unenlightened hydroelectric development. The North Fork has been forever altered by the presence of numerous power dams and powerhouses. In some places the fishing has improved as a result of the hydropower operations, but the overall effect of the hydroelectric development has been to destroy what was once a world famous trout fishery.

Perhaps "destroy" is too strong of a word. Trout can be found in the North Fork from Lake Oroville to Lake Almanor. The river is particularly good immediately above and below Belden Forebay. Access is easy in most places, as there are numerous pull-outs along the highway. The river is primarily a wild-trout stream. The river is only stocked near the campgrounds along the road to Belden Forebay. Unlike many rivers with hydroelectric projects, anglers don't need to worry about changes in water releases, as the gates on the dams are locked in place during the summer months.

Although trout can be found in the North Fork from Lake Oroville to Lake Almanor, the operations of the various hydropower facilities affect local populations of fish. Rock Creek, Cresta, and Poe, the three power dams in the canyon along Highway 70, affect the river the most. Trout migrate up and downstream throughout the year to feed, spawn, and find shelter. These large dams block seasonal migrations of fish, and also block access to prime spawning tributaries. The dams also reduce the amount of water downstream to a small fraction of historic

The giant boulders of the North Fork Feather River provide unique casting and maneuvering challenges.

KAREN HARRIS BOONE

The Feather River Canyon is famous for its overlapping railroad and highway bridges.

flows. Low flows translate into low dissolved oxygen levels and lack of suitable habitat. Water temperatures have also been elevated by larger, shallow reservoirs upstream which serve as heat sinks for the sun's energy.

With the high water temperatures and low dissolved oxygen levels, prime fishing spots become pretty obvious in the summer. Trout can be found wherever there is moving water, since riffles aerate the water. There is a lot of slow water in the North Fork that isn't very productive. In most places there are at best three or four really good pools you can fish in any one spot because they are surrounded by long stretches of slow water. Don't let this discourage you; there are many miles of river to fish, and you just have to keep moving. Other obvious places to fish are where tributaries enter the river.

Attractor dries and searching nymph patterns produce well, although occasionally a hatch of green drakes or smaller mayflies will come off that demands closer replication. The trout key in on adult stoneflies in the spring. If you don't have any big adult stonefly patterns, try floating a Woolly Bugger. Hopper patterns work very well in the fall.

The Flood of January 1997 caused incredible damage
to the area's roads, bridges, and trails.

When nymphing be sure to use a long leader to get the fly down on the bottom. The massive boulders that make up the streambed of the North Fork make for some very deep pockets. During summer, the trout will be hugging the bottom.

The revitalization of the trout fishery in the North Fork will take many years. As this book goes to press, CalTrout and other conservation groups are fighting for significant fishery enhancements in Federal Energy Regulatory Commission meetings, as the Cresta and Rock Creek hydroelectric projects are currently up for relicensing. Although this is an incredible opportunity to improve the fishery, progress will be difficult, and will require the help of many volunteers. I urge all readers to support CalTrout and other organizations that are trying to improve our fisheries. Also remember that the wild trout of the North Fork are true survivors. Please show them the respect they deserve and practice catch and release.

While you're driving through the Feather River Canyon be sure to notice the various highway and railroad bridges. The railroad was completed in 1909, and the railroad surveyors naturally chose the best route through the canyon. When the Feather River Highway was being built during the late twenties and thirties, the highway surveyors were given a much tougher task. Throughout most of the canyon the highway and railroad are on opposite sides of the canyon. At Tobin and Pulga the highway and railroad bridges cross in the same place, although not in the same fashion. At Tobin the railroad bridge is above the highway bridge, and at Pulga the railroad bridge is far below the highway bridge. Be sure to keep an eye out for rocks and deer while driving the canyon.

Highway 70 provides easy access to the North Fork Feather River.

Poe Powerhouse to Poe Dam

Poe Powerhouse, the lowest powerhouse on the North Fork, marks the beginning of Lake Oroville. The riverbed of the North Fork Feather River is very rough in this area, so it is difficult to fish more than a handful of pools in any given location. As with much of the North Fork, wading won't get you very far, as the water is too deep. You're better off wearing a good pair of rock-hopping shoes.

The best times to fish this lowest part of the river are in the spring and fall. This section is fishable as soon as the spring runoff recedes to the point where it's no longer spilling over Poe Dam. There aren't as many trout in this part of the river, but the average size is over a foot. The best places to access the river are at Poe Powerhouse, Bardees Bar, and Pulga, which is right below Poe Dam. You can access Poe Powerhouse and Bardees Bar by taking Detlow Road or Big Bend Road, which branch off Highway 70 about seven miles west of the Pulga Bridge. 4WD is recommended for the road to Bardees Bar. There is a lot of frogwater near Pulga, but you will encounter better water by hiking up- or downstream. The area immediately below the dam can be accessed via a pullout on the highway, but the railroad tracks that run through Pulga offer good access upstream or downstream.

Due to the heat at these lower elevations during the summer, concentrate your angling effort in the early morning and late-evening hours. It is legal to fish here during the winter, and the fishing can be good when the stream isn't blown out. Large stoneflies emerge all winter long, so don't be afraid to try a big stonefly nymph or dry. Hopper patterns work very well here in the fall.

Cresta Powerhouse to Cresta Dam

Cresta Powerhouse is just upstream from Poe Reservoir, and carries water diverted from Cresta Dam upstream. This is the most de-watered stretch of the North Fork. On the one hand, the low water makes the stream easy to fish in this area, but on the other hand, there would be ten times as many fish if the river was restored to its historic capacity.

Concentrations of fish can be found wherever there is moving, oxygenated water.

Some of the best places to fish here are immediately above Cresta Powerhouse, near the Shady Rest rest stop, and from the confluence with Grizzly Creek on up to Cresta Dam. Although there are times when it is necessary to dredge the bottom with nymphs, the fish in this section will usually rise to dries. Elk Hair Caddis, Goddard's Caddis, and other caddis patterns work very well in this stretch.

Grizzly Creek

Aside from being one of the most popular rock-climbing spots in the Plumas National Forest, Grizzly Creek is also one of the largest tributaries to the North Fork Feather River. Good fish move up into the lower part of Grizzly Creek to escape the high water temperatures in the North Fork Feather River, and a lot of good fish wash out of Grizzly Forebay upstream

A good Grizzly Creek rainbow.

in the spring. The lower part of the creek can be accessed only from the highway. The best way to fish this creek is to wet-wade. It's usually hot enough in the canyon that you'll want to jump in anyway. Fish attractor dries like Humpies and Stimulators. Grizzly Creek is pretty steep, so you can only fish about a quarter mile of it from the highway without doing some serious rock climbing. Grizzly Forebay and Grizzly Creek above the forebay are described later in the book as part of the Bucks Lake Area.

Rock Creek Powerhouse to Rock Creek Dam

Rock Creek Dam is the uppermost dam on the North Fork in the canyon section that flows alongside Highway 70. This is the first dam in the system to handle water from the East Branch of the North Fork, which conflues with the North Fork several miles upstream at Gansner Bar. Due to the extensive water manipulation on the true North Fork, the East Branch now carries more water than the North Fork. The East Branch also carries an incredible amount of silt during the spring runoff, and the reservoir backed up by Rock Creek Dam has lost approximately 50 percent of its original storage capacity due to siltation.

The tailwater section below Rock Creek Dam holds a fair number of trout but suffers from low flows and high water temperatures. The best stretch is immediately below Bucks Creek Powerhouse, which is located about a mile upstream from Rock Creek Powerhouse, at the upstream end of Cresta Reservoir. Bucks Creek Powerhouse was completed in 1928 by the Great Western Power Company. With a head of 2,562 feet, Bucks Creek Powerhouse had the highest head of any power-house in the Western Hemisphere. The head is the drop in elevation from the water source to the powerhouse. Rock Creek Powerhouse was commissioned in 1950 with a head of 481 feet. Both powerhouses are now operated by PG&E.

Bucks Creek Powerhouse contributes much-needed cold, oxygenated water to the river. Since there is more water in this section it is necessary to add a little extra weight to your nymphs. Use beadhead nymphs or nymphs with bead-chain eyes. I have also witnessed better mayfly hatches in this part of the river than in other parts. Come prepared with parachute mayfly patterns of assorted colors and sizes. In the river above Bucks Creek Powerhouse, caddis, stonefly, and searching nymph patterns work best. Stoneflies emerge soon after the runoff water recedes and the stream resumes its normal summer flow, and caddis hatches provide action throughout most of the season.

There are fish to be had in the river immediately above Rock Creek Reservoir, but this stretch doesn't compare to the river between Gansner Bar and Belden Forebay. However, Yellow Creek is good where it empties into the river at Belden. There is a rest stop at Belden where a relic of the gold mining days is on display. The Eby Stamp Mill has five stamps and was used at the White Lily mine near Seneca. This mill served for thirty-nine years until the mine failed in 1937.

Gansner Bar to Belden Forebay

The river forks at Gansner Bar, with the North Fork heading off to Lake Almanor and the East Branch heading east to the confluence of Indian and Spanish creeks. This stretch, between Gansner Bar and Belden Forebay, is arguably the best part of the river. Anglers can have their choice between stocked and wild fish, as the river is stocked heavily near the campgrounds, but wild rainbows predominate upstream. This is one of the most popular picks for Opening Day since the stream is usually nice and low coming out of Belden Forebay.

This part of the river holds a lot of productive pocket water, and is very well-suited to short-line nymphing techniques. You'll have to work hard for your fish here, though, since blackberry bushes and poison oak line the banks of the stream, and there are many fly-eating trees and bushes. The stream can be fished from the bank in spots, but you'll be limiting your success if those are the only places you fish. The best way to fish this river is with neoprene waders, stream cleats, and a wading staff. That way you can forge up through the middle of the stream instead of dealing with the brush on the edges. You can also position yourself in the best spot to make your cast if you're actually in the stream. Wet-wading is often a good choice when temperatures soar in the summer.

Nymphs work best in this part of the river, although there are hatches of mayflies, caddisflies, and little yellow stones that will bring the fish up. Stoneflies hatch profusely in May and June, and can be imitated with a black Rubberleg Stone. Beadhead Bird's Nests, Prince Nymphs, and Hare's Ears work very well throughout the season, and grasshopper patterns will attract some attention in the fall. In the evening, it is often rewarding to prospect with a big attractor dry fly even if no fish are seen rising.

Flowers adorn the North Fork Feather River in the spring.

DANGER
WATER MAY BE DISCHARGED IN
THIS AREA AT ANY INSTANT IT IS
FROM THIS . . . . . TO THIS
IN 3 SECONDS

Use caution and common sense when fishing near any hydroelectric operation.

Belden Forebay (2986 feet) to Lake Almanor (4482 feet)

Belden Forebay was built as part of the Feather River Stairway of Power. Caribou #1 and #2 Powerhouses empty into the upper part of the forebay, which also serves to divert water to the Belden Powerhouse. Caribou #1 is one of the oldest powerhouses in the Feather River Canyon. Three generators (more would be added later) began turning out 73,000 kilowatts in 1921. The power went to the San Francisco Bay Area. Pacific Gas & Electric took over the plant in 1930. Caribou #2 was completed in 1958.

The operation of these two powerhouses creates a very artificial and interesting set of circumstances for the trout and other fish in the Forebay. Quite a few fish from Butt Valley Reservoir become entrained in the penstocks that feed the powerhouses, and are subsequently chopped up in the turbines and released into the upper end of the forebay. These unfortunate fish are eaten by the fish in the forebay. The fish in the forebay are so dependent on the operation of the powerhouse that they will move up in mass from the forebay the moment the powerhouse cranks up.

A fast-sinking fly line is necessary to get your fly down to the bottom in the swift current below the powerhouse. Alaskan carcass flies are a good bet for imitating the chunks of fish flesh that are ejected from the powerhouse, as are pond smelt imitations. Zonkers and other flashy streamers will also produce. The main problem is the unpredictability of the powerhouse operation. Good times to be fishing are immediately after the powerhouse turns on and when the powerhouse is operating at low capacity. To further complicate things, the water level in the forebay changes rapidly due to inflow from the powerhouses and outflow to Belden Powerhouse downstream. The fluctuating water level drastically changes the hydrology of the inlet.

The operation of the powerhouses also seems to affect the North Fork above the forebay. The river above the forebay is a very temperamental fishery, as fish regularly migrate between the river and the forebay. The river here is about the same size as below Belden Forebay, but is crystal clear and the rocks are extremely slippery. The insect life is pretty phenomenal in this part of the stream. I have seen more intense hatches here than on any other part of the North Fork. The smaller trout are usually eager to rise to dries, but the bigger fish aren't as easy. Try fishing a nymph through some of the pockets and you'll connect with some larger fish. The last three hours of daylight are the best time to fish this stream.

To access the North Fork immediately above Belden Forebay you must hike in from the parking lot at Belden Forebay. To get around Caribou Powerhouse #1 you have to walk on a railed metal walkway attached to the powerhouse wall. The walkway was built only several feet above the pipes which release the water from the turbines. Once you get around the powerhouse, a good trail follows the river upstream for a couple of miles. There are two very picturesque (and bouncy!) footbridges on this trail. Be sure to fish the first pool where the stream empties into the forebay, immediately upstream from the powerhouse. Large fish from the forebay will occasionally hold in this pool and can be surprisingly easy to catch.

The North Fork can also be accessed upstream at Seneca and again below the dam at Lake Almanor. There are also some old 4WD roads that lead down to the river. The fishing is generally good in this part of the river, although it would be much better with increased flows from Lake Almanor. You better have a Forest Service map if you plan on exploring this part of the river.

Yellow Creek

Yellow Creek is one of California's precious few spring creeks. Well-known for its large browns early in this century, Yellow Creek suffered for many years due to unrestricted cattle grazing. In 1971, CalTrout proposed that the Humbug Valley portion of the creek be added to the brand new California Wild Trout Program. Volunteers fenced off a half-mile portion of the creek as an experiment in restoration. Instream improvements were made and everyone waited to see what would happen. In just five years, the brown trout population increased 600 percent, and the decision was made to restore and fence off the remaining portion of the creek that flows through Humbug Valley.

Yellow Creek is one of California's precious few spring creeks.

Once the habitat was restored, the only thing keeping the trout population from recovering was anglers. With Yellow Creek gaining in popularity, 10- to 20-inch fish became rare due to overharvest. This size gap put the population at risk, as the 10- to 20-inch fish account for the majority of the spawning production. CalTrout pushed for and won a minimum size limit of 16 inches at Yellow Creek in 1984. To protect the larger fish, the regulations were changed again in 1990 to allow the angler two fish, maximum size ten inches. These regulations govern the entire Humbug Valley portion of the creek, from Big Springs to the marker at the end of the valley. The normal five-fish limit applies downstream in the canyon section of Yellow Creek.

The restoration effort at Yellow Creek has been very successful. Ten- to sixteen-inch fish are the norm, and bigger fish are caught frequently. Willows are reclaiming and strengthening the banks of the stream. Aquatic insect life is impressive, with hatches coming off year round. Perhaps most importantly, the stream is now separated from the cows by a beautiful split-cedar fence.

Fly selections for Yellow Creek should include small mayfly, caddis, midge, and terrestrial patterns. Mayfly spinners, Mathews' Sparkle Duns, Quiggly Cripples, Parachute Adams', Blue Wing Olives, Pale Morning Duns, and Griffith's Gnats in size 16 to 22 are appropriate. Emerger patterns such as the RS-2 and CDC Transitional Dun can also be effective. Small caddisflies emerge at certain times of the year and can be imitated with an Elk Hair Caddis, size 18-20. Stoneflies are prevalent in the lower canyon. Once in a while you may spot a fish at Yellow Creek that is feeding subsurface. Small (size 18-20) Pheasant Tail Nymphs pitched gently upstream from these fish and allowed to sink will often do the trick.

As with any spring creek, anglers must be very careful when fishing Yellow Creek. The best times are mid-morning and evening. Mayflies hatch at these times and the trout will be feeding on the surface. On a calm, overcast day the fish may rise all day long. The best strategy for fishing Yellow Creek is to walk along the creek and look for rising fish. Listen carefully for rises up or downstream. Rising fish can be found from Big Springs, where the creek bubbles out of the ground, all the way down to the end of Humbug Valley, well over two miles of stream. A pair of hip boots is ideal footwear for fishing Yellow Creek. They will allow you to cross the creek and trudge through the soggy pastures without getting wet. Watch out for sinkholes. Light rods, 4-weight and under, are ideal. Nine- to twelve-foot leaders are necessary, and should be tapered down to 6X tippet.

Yellow Creek is most easily reached from Highway 89 near Lake Almanor. Traveling north on 89, there is a turnoff marked "Yellow Creek Campground" about 7.8 miles from the dam. Punch your odometer as you turn off. At 0.6 miles there is a fork, stay left. At 1.6, 2.1, 3.9, and 5.0 miles there are four-way intersections—go straight through each one. At 1.9 miles the road crosses Butt Creek. At 7.4 miles you reach Humbug Valley, and you can take a left towards the Yellow Creek Campground. This is a beautiful place to stay when you fish Yellow Creek. There are twelve units, and the campground is very neat and well-kept.

Butt Valley Reservoir (4142 feet)

Butt Valley Reservoir is arguably one of the best trout lakes in California. Constructed by the Great Western Power Company as part of the Lake Almanor hydroelectric project, this lake is famous for its average eighteen-inch trout. These large rainbows are of the fast-growing Eagle Lake trout variety, and they're all wild. Large browns and smallmouth bass also provide interesting angling opportunities.

Most of the fishing action is concentrated near the estuary at the north end of the lake. There is a long, artificial peninsula that bisects the estuary, with Butt Creek on one side and the water from the Butt Creek Powerhouse on the other side. The peninsula is a very popular fishing spot. Both sides of the peninsula are very productive.

The water on the west side of the peninsula often holds pond smelt that have been crippled or stunned during their trip through the tunnel and powerhouse. These tiny baitfish inhabit Lake Almanor and Butt Valley Reservoir, and the trout feast on them when they are being ejected from the powerhouse. The most popular fly for imitating the crippled baitfish is Milt's Pond Smelt, created by local guide Milt Jensen.

White marabou flesh-flies also work well. The summer months usually provide the best action on pond smelt imitations.

On the other side of the peninsula, plenty of cool water flows into the lake from spring-fed Butt Creek. Trout move into this inlet in the summer when temperatures in the main body of the lake become uncomfortably high. Pheasant Tails, black Bird's Nests, Princes, and A. P. Nymphs in sizes 12 to 18 work well fished under an indicator in this inlet. Streamers such as the Woolly Bugger, Zonker, and the Janssen Leech also work well when allowed to sink and then stripped in slowly.

Although the fishing in Butt Creek estuary is the most dependable, Butt Valley Reservoir is most famous for its annual hatch of giant *Hexagenia* mayflies. These mammoth mayflies attract the attention of even the largest trout. The hatch usually starts mid-June and can last well through the month of July. The hexes emerge in the late evening in the main body of the lake. The nymphs become active in the late afternoon, and they begin to emerge in the last 45 minutes before dark. Like grasshopper or damsel nymph patterns, there are hundreds of different *Hexagenia* patterns. Two of the best are Milt Jensen's *Hexagenia* nymph and *Hexagenia* paradun. Troll a nymph pattern slowly on an intermediate or full-sink line until you see hexes on the water, then switch to a dry. A visit to one of the local fly shops listed in Appendix B should provide you with a good sampling of Hex patterns. They are also the people to ask whether the hatch is on or not. *Hexagenia* devotees can also catch the hatch at Lake Almanor and Fall River (tributary to the Pit River).

Butt Valley Reservoir was drained in the spring of 1996 to facilitate repairs to the dam, which would have been vulnerable to failure in the event of an earthquake. The construction was completed in November 1997, and the lake has filled and appears to be fishing well. Butt Valley Reservoir can be reached from Caribou or Lake Almanor. On Highway 89 near Lake Almanor there is a marked turnoff for Butt Valley Reservoir. You'll need a Forest Service map to find your way in from Caribou. There are two large campgrounds on the lake, Cool Springs and Ponderosa Flat. Don't overlook Butt Creek above the reservoir. It's a good stream with a mixed bag of rainbows and browns.

East Branch of the North Fork Feather River

The East Branch of the North Fork comes into being at the confluence of Spanish Creek and Indian Creek and flows over 10 miles along Highway 70 before joining into the North Fork of the Feather River. Unlike the North Fork, the East Branch has yet to be tamed by hydroelectric dams, but still suffers from elevated water temperatures. The water in Indian Creek warms up considerably as it travels through Genesee and Indian Valley. This warm water is dumped into the East Branch, joining somewhat cooler water from Spanish Creek. The result is an environment slightly on the warm side for trout.

Like the lower North Fork, obvious places to fish include pocket water, heads of pools, and places where tributaries enter the river. Much work has been done recently to construct fish ladders to help fish access spawning grounds in tributaries that were blocked by highway and railroad culverts. Hopefully improved spawning conditions and upstream erosion control projects will help to improve the trout fishery in the East Branch.

Spanish Creek

Spanish Creek is one of the better early season streams in the Plumas National Forest. It's usually high but fishable on Opening Day, and in really good shape by the first of June. This stream produces a lot of good browns each year. Spanish Creek has also been stocked with rainbow trout in recent years. The fish are stocked near the park in Quincy. Another good stretch is downstream from Quincy, below Oakland Camp. Spanish Creek can also be accessed at Spanish Creek campground, which is near the Highway 70/89 bridge over Spanish Creek. Farther downstream, Spanish Falls is a good fishing and swimming spot. Fish can be found in Spanish Creek all the way up to Meadow Valley. Some good small-stream fly fishing can also be found in the tributaries to Spanish Creek on the road from Quincy to Bucks Lake.

Bucks Lake Area

The Bucks Lake area is not only rich in fishing possibilities, but is rich in history as well. Bucks Valley was first settled in the fall of 1850 by Horace Bucklin and Francis Walker. Bucklin, commonly called "Buck," named the valley Buck's Ranch. That same year a black mountain man by the name of James Beckwourth discovered the lowest pass over the Sierra Nevada. The wagon trail he established quickly became a popular immigrant route into California. The Beckwourth Trail, as it came to be known, led from Beckwourth Pass near the present site of Hallelujah Junction to Bidwell Bar, which is now deep under the waters of Lake Oroville. Buck's Ranch was a popular wagon stop along the route, and prospered so long as immigrants continued to use Beckwourth's route. The trail declined in popularity in 1855 as better routes through the Sierra became developed. The Beckwourth Trail is now adorned with numerous historic markers, many of which can be found near Bucks Lake. A complete guide to the historical markers along the Beckwourth Trail can be found at the Quincy Museum.

Buck's Ranch gave way to Bucks Lake in 1928. Bucks Lake dam was built to store water for the Bucks Creek Powerhouse in the Feather River Canyon. The project was started in 1925 by the Feather River Power Company, which sold out to the Great Western Power Company prior to the project's completion in 1928. Grizzly Forebay, Lower Bucks Lake, and Three Lakes were all part of the same hydroelectric project. The Bucks Creek Project is now an integral part of PG&E's Feather River Stairway of Power. The reservoirs created as part of the Bucks Creek Project now provide excellent angling opportunities, as do the many free-flowing streams and natural lakes in the area.

The Bucks Lake area can be reached via the Oroville-Quincy Highway from Oroville or Quincy. This road is now fully paved, although there are some very narrow and windy sections on parts of both roads. Bucks Lake is 17 miles from Quincy and about 45 miles from Oroville. Visitors can find accommodations at Bucks Lake Lodge or Bucks Lakeshore Resort. Both offer housekeeping cabins, and Bucks Lake Lodge also offers a small motel and a new bed & breakfast. There are also numerous campgrounds in the area. Mill Creek, Sundew, and Haskins campgrounds are right on Bucks Lake, and the nearby Whitehorse, Grizzly Creek, and Lower Bucks campgrounds are also popular. The three campgrounds on the lake fill up on many weekends during the summer. They're occupied on a first come, first serve basis, so plan your vacations accordingly. Those same campgrounds are usually less than half full during the week.

If you're interested in hiking in to some of the lakes and streams in the area you should definitely pick up a map of the Bucks Lake Wilderness. It's a brand-new topo map put out by the USFS, and it's much easier than packing along several smaller 7.5-minute quadrangles.

Bucks Lake (5155 feet)

Bucks Lake is one of the most popular fishing areas in the Plumas National Forest. The lake is home to five species of salmonids, including rainbow, brown, brook, and lake trout, and kokanee salmon. Having marginal natural reproduction among the trout species, Bucks Lake is stocked several times throughout the season by the California Department of Fish and Game. Catchable rainbows and brookies are planted from Memorial Day to Labor Day, and fingerling mackinaw (lake trout) are planted annually. Brown trout fingerlings are also planted periodically.

Water is released from Bucks Lake according to a delicate balancing act: the immediate need for power versus the need to store water for future power generation. In recent years the lake has been kept full until August or September. The lake is drawn down in the fall, exposing the shallows and preventing the growth of significant aquatic vegetation. Since the shallows provide little nourishment, the fish concentrate near the inlet streams throughout the year. The inlets of Bucks, Haskins, Mill, and Right Hand Branch Mill Creek provide the majority of the fly-fishing action at Bucks Lake.

In spring, when the fishing is at its peak, it is difficult to fish the inlets from shore because there is little room to backcast. In Mill Creek and Bucks Creek you might be able to get a decent roll cast, but you'd be much better off fishing from a float tube or boat. Big nymphs work well in the spring, as do streamers and Woolly Buggers. Sink-tip lines are helpful this time of year, as the trout cruise in about three to eight feet of water. Mayflies and midges hatch profusely in the spring at Bucks, and can be imitated with parachute mayfly patterns and Griffith's Gnats.

By July the water warms and the inflow from the tributaries drops considerably, demanding a small change in tactics. The fish still congregate near the inlets, but they often hold in slightly deeper water in the old creek channels. Cast sink-tip or full-sink lines towards these old streambeds, which are often visible. Let the fly sink down near the bottom before stripping it in slowly. Patterns that work well in this situation are Prince Nymphs, Marabou Damsels, Zug Bugs, and Pheasant Tail Nymphs in sizes 10-14, and Woolly Buggers. If you don't catch fish near the inlet, slowly work your way away from the inlet, following the submerged streambed as closely as possible.

Due to high surface temperatures, August and early September are tough for the fly-fisher at Bucks Lake. Air and water temperatures start to drop by the end of September, signaling the beginning of fall and the return of good fly fishing. October and November are very good to the fly-fisher at Bucks Lake. The inlets are still very productive, but fish can now be found all over the lake, cruising the shoreline in search of food. Large fish reappear this time of year, and catches of large browns and holdover rainbows are common. Shore fishing works just as well as float tubing this time of year. Small to medium-sized searching nymphs work well when cast to likely spots or to sighted fish.

Lower Bucks Lake (5027 feet)

Lower Bucks Lake can be found immediately below Bucks Lake. This reservoir was constructed to collect water from Bucks Lake and Three Lakes and to divert it to Grizzly Forebay. A lot of water moves through this reservoir, keeping it nice and cool even during the hottest summer months. Lower Bucks is a nice alternative to Bucks Lake in August and September when the fish in the upper lake have headed for the depths.

This desolate scene at Lower Bucks Lake is a common sight at area reservoirs, which are frequently drawn down according to hydroelectric power demand.

The water level at Lower Bucks Lake fluctuates according to the demand for hydroelectric power, and you must change your tactics accordingly. Most of the fish can be found cruising the shorelines, and this is where you want to fish. One of the best spots is the big cove near the makeshift boat ramp. There is a lot of structure in the form of stumps and submerged brush in this cove. Fish Prince Nymphs on a slow, irregular retrieve near this structure or over the old creekbed. This technique works well all around the lake. When the water is high a float tube is beneficial as backcasting room is scarce. Paddle out into the lake and cast in towards the shoreline. When the water level drops it is possible to fish from shore or to wade out into the water and fish from a stump.

Midge hatches account for the majority of the surface-feeding trout on Lower Bucks Lake. Brown trout dominate this lake, and they become very selective when feeding on midges. These midges are often too small for imitation, but Griffith's Gnats and midge pupa patterns in very small sizes often work. When there are no fish feeding on the surface at Lower Bucks, troll an Olive Beadhead Woolly Bugger on a floating or sink-tip line.

Water from Three Lakes empties into Lower Bucks Lake through a pipe on the north side of the lake near the dam. This is one of the best places to fish in the spring and early summer, as the fish stack up to feed on whatever goodies come through the pipe. Although most anything will work here, including dry flies drifted on the current, big Zonker streamers seem to work best. Stand on either side of the pipe and cast across the current. Let the fly swing an arc through the current and then pull it in with a moderate stop-and-go retrieve. The fish usually hit on the swing, but they will occasionally strike on the retrieve. Big fish can be found here.

There is a makeshift boat ramp at Lower Bucks which is well-suited for trailers, and there is a campground for self-contained vehicles (no water available) on the lake.

Grizzly Forebay (4320 feet)

Grizzly Forebay is one of the few places where the water stays cool throughout the year. There is a new powerhouse at the upper end of the forebay that dumps in cold water from the bottom of Lower Bucks Lake. Thanks to this hydroelectric meddling, Grizzly Forebay remains very cool even when surface temperatures at most reservoirs are well into the 70s. These cool temperatures make this lake a prime fly-fishing destination during the hottest summer months.

Grizzly Forebay is very similar to Lower Bucks Lake, and can be fished in the same manner. The main difference is that Grizzly Forebay is about five to ten degrees cooler than Lower Bucks. The cold water comes in at the powerhouse, and I have observed that the fish feed only away from the powerhouse, in the warmer part of the lake near the dam. The water ejected from the powerhouse is in the low- to mid-fifties, but the temperature rises five to ten degrees at the other end of the forebay.

Fly selections for Grizzly Forebay should include Olive Beadhead Woolly Buggers, Griffith's Gnats, and parachute mayflies in the smaller sizes. Large flying ants hatch in May and June. Although there are times when the lake is down and you can stalk rising fish from the shoreline, a float tube or pram comes in handy when the lake is full and shore-fishing is next to impossible.

Grizzly Forebay is most easily reached from the Oro-Quincy Highway. The turnoff is about two miles west of the Bucks Lake Dam Road turnoff. The road is paved most of the way. There isn't an actual boat ramp at Grizzly Forebay, but it is possible (if somewhat difficult) to launch an aluminum boat at the end of the road.

Grizzly Creek (above Grizzly Forebay)

Grizzly Creek is one of the prettiest small streams in the Plumas National Forest. For years, water from Lower Bucks Lake was released into the creek several miles above Grizzly Forebay. This enormous amount of water brought a lot of big fish up from Grizzly Forebay, and limits of large rainbows and browns were not uncommon. However, a new powerhouse at Grizzly Forebay was completed in the last few years, and the water is no longer released upstream from the forebay.

Although the creek has been left with its meager natural flow, the decades of high flows have left Grizzly Creek with a nicely polished

Wild rainbows and browns can be found in Grizzly Creek, near Bucks Lake.

streambed. The water carved out nice pools that now support wild populations of rainbows and browns. The stream suffers from a lot of angling pressure, but fish move up from the forebay throughout the season, replacing the fish that have been taken. To access Grizzly Creek take the turnoff to Grizzly Forebay from the Oro-Quincy Highway. The road is a couple hundred feet above the creek so be careful negotiating the steep slope. Most fly patterns will work, although the trout here have a particular fondness for Brown Bivisibles. Montana Stones and other large nymphs work well in the early season.

Silver Lake (5800 feet)

Silver Lake is one of the prettiest lakes in the Plumas National Forest. At one time a very small natural lake, it was raised by a dam to provide water storage for hydraulic mining. The eastern end of the lake is rather shallow, while the western end, where the original lake was located, is deeper. In the spring fish can be caught in the shallow end, which is also nearest to the road. As the water warms throughout the season, fish move into the deeper end.

This scenic lake is well-suited to float tube, pram, or canoe fly fishing. There is a launch ramp but trailers are not advisable on the road in to the lake. Brook trout are the main fare at Silver Lake, although the occasional rainbow is caught as well. The brook trout from Silver Lake are the most beautiful representatives of their species I have ever seen. They also reach pretty good size, with ten- to twelve-inch fish being very common. Silver Lake is 6.4 miles from Meadow Valley on a dirt road passable to most 2WD vehicles. Silver Lake also serves as the trailhead for Gold Lake and the Pacific Crest Trail.

Bucks Lake Wilderness

The Bucks Lake Wilderness was established by the California Wilderness Act of 1984. It features numerous small creeks and lakes, steep granite cliffs, quaking bogs, and large stands of Red Firs. There are beautiful overlooks of Bucks Lake and the Feather River Canyon, the bottom of which is nearly a vertical mile from the peak of Mount Pleasant. Several trails cross the 21,000-acre wilderness, with the Pacific Crest Trail serving as the main artery. Trails branch off from the Pacific Crest Trail to Kellogg Lake, Silver and Gold Lake, Three Lakes, and Bucks Lake via the Mill Creek and Right Hand Branch Mill Creek trails. Several lakes in the wilderness hold trout, including Three Lakes, Gold Lake, and Lost Lake. These lakes are stocked by air periodically with rainbow, brown, and brook trout fingerlings. Two tributaries to Bucks Lake also flow through the wilderness. Mill Creek and Right Hand Branch Mill Creek are full of small but eager rainbows, brookies, and browns. These streams are only open from July 1 to September 30 to protect spawning fish. Although a permit is not required to enter the Bucks Lake Wilderness, there are registration boxes at each trailhead. Please fill out a registration form when you enter the wilderness; the registration data provides the Forest Service with vital information for managing the wilderness.

Gold Lake (5950 feet)

Gold Lake is home to some fair-sized brook trout. This is a very pretty lake, and also rather deep. I wouldn't bother fly fishing this one without a float tube, though, since the shoreline is only easily accessible in one spot. The fish seem to congregate along the weedy shoreline on the west side of the lake. The water is shallower and there is more insect activity there.

Gold Lake is 1.5 miles from the trailhead at the dam on the east side of Silver Lake. Trail time is 45 minutes to an hour either way. The trail crosses an old aqueduct which used to carry water from Gold Lake to Silver Lake. This trail also allows access to the Pacific Crest Trail via the Granite Gap Trail, which splits off about halfway to Gold Lake. The Granite Gap Trail is 0.9 miles long, and also can be used to hike to Mud Lake and Rock Lake, two scenic but fishless little lakes. Both the Gold Lake and Granite Gap trails are great for family hikes and picnics, and Gold Lake and Rock Lake are popular swimming holes.

Three Lakes (6080 feet)

Three Lakes can produce some really nice brookies and browns for the effective float-tuber. Three Lakes is actually only two lakes, since the lowest lake was raised with a dam and connected by a small channel to the second lake. These two lakes hold the best fish, but the third lake is good, too. It's also the prettiest of the three lakes, by far. Three Lakes is a great float-tube destination since you can drive right up to the first lake. The lakes are fairly deep, and fish can be caught using small Woolly Buggers attached to sink-tip lines.

Three Lakes is twelve miles from Bucks Lake on a very unpleasant 4WD road. Three Lakes is right on the Pacific Crest Trail, and is a good trailhead for a hike to Lost Lake or Kellogg Lake.

Lost Lake (5880 feet)

Lost Lake is a beautiful little gem tucked away against a steep granite slope in between two small glacial moraines. This is a hike-in destination that is seldom fished. As you hike around the steep south side of the lake to the only passable campsite over on the north side, you will no doubt see several good-sized brookies feeding against the steep bank. The best way to fish this lake is by float tube. The fish will move into the shallows in the morning and evening, but during the day they hold on the north side in the deeper water. There's so much brush that it's really difficult to fish that south side from shore. If you want to fish the best water, you really need to pack-in a float tube. The lake is really too far for a day hike so you'll be packing the float tube on top of all your camping gear. The hike in is no picnic, either.

The shortest route into Lost Lake is from Three Lakes, although it can also be reached from the Mill Creek trailhead near Bucks Lake or from Silver Lake. Hike along the Pacific Crest Trail until you're just west of Mount Pleasant. I strongly suggest that you buy the Bucks Lake Wilderness topo map before going on this trip. I've found that it's best to follow the ridge on the east side of the lake down until you're only a couple hundred feet above the lake. Then make your way as best you can to the south side of the lake, then follow the little trail around the west side to the north side, where there is a decent campsite. Avoid the shorter route around the east side of the lake, since it is very brushy. Leave the shorts at home for this hike; a good pair of lightweight pants will save you from the brush.

Middle Fork of the Feather River

In the eyes of the angler, the Middle Fork is the uncontested king among the forks of the Feather River. There are over 35 miles of wild, nearly inaccessible water between Lake Oroville and Nelson Creek, and another 20 miles of productive water above Nelson Creek. In 1968, the Middle Fork was granted Wild & Scenic status when Congress passed the National Wild & Scenic Rivers Act. Draining a 1,240-square-mile area, the Middle Fork Feather River is possibly the finest free-flowing trout stream remaining in California.

An angler battles a feisty rainbow in the Wild and Scenic Canyon of the Middle Fork Feather River.

The Middle Fork originates in the Sierra Valley Channels east of Portola. It flows westward roughly following Highway 70 until the town of Sloat, where it falls under the designation of the English Bar Scenic River Zone. There are several vehicle accesses in this area. At Nelson Creek the river begins its journey through the Upper Canyon Wild River Zone. With the exception of three rough jeep trails, the river is only accessible by foot in this area. The Wild River Zone is interrupted by another Scenic River Zone at Milsap Bar, where there is a vehicle bridge

Two old bridge pilings adorn the banks of the Middle Fork Feather River below its confluence with Bear Creek.

Numerous trout can often be seen rising in the tailout of the large pool below this impressive suspension bridge, where the Hartman Bar National Recreation Trail crosses the Middle Fork Feather River.

across the river. Below Milsap Bar is the Bald Rock Canyon Wild River Zone, again only accessible by foot.

Fly fishing becomes productive in the Middle Fork around mid-June as the runoff begins to recede. The best part of the Middle Fork is between Nelson Creek and Lake Oroville. Once the runoff period is over, the fishing in this section is consistently good until the end of the season in mid-November. Fifteen- to twenty-fish days are average, and most fish fall in the ten- to fourteen-inch category. Below Milsap Bar the average fish is about fourteen inches, but the numbers of fish aren't as high. I have found that the smaller fish will rise to dry flies, while most of the larger fish are taken on nymphs or streamers. Hopper patterns will also bring up good fish, especially between July and October.

Dry-fly fishing is great during June, July, and August. There are usually several hatches going on at any given time, so the fish rarely feed selectively. Yellow Humpies, Elk Hair Caddis, and other attractor patterns work well. There is one hatch of creamy mayflies that comes off between mid-June and mid-July that requires close imitation. This hatch can be matched with a Fall River Special or Light Cahill in sizes 12 to 16. Midges also hatch in abundance on the Middle Fork, and can be imitated with small Griffith's Gnats.

When the fish won't come up to the surface on the Middle Fork they can usually be easily had with nymphs. The river is well-suited to indicator nymphing, but there are some pocket water areas where indicatorless nymphing is more effective. This technique is detailed in Part Three and will help you reach fish where the water is either too fast or deep for indicator nymphing to be effective. Hopper patterns and small Muddler Minnows can also be used to get the attention of non-rising trout.

Accessing the Middle Fork

There are many trails and roads that access the Middle Fork of the Feather River. I have organized these accesses into four areas, starting from Lake Oroville and moving upstream. I have written a general description for each area, followed by detailed descriptions of each of the river accesses in that particular area. For each river access, I've listed several important factors, including length of trail, directions to the trailhead, time in and out, condition of road and trail, and other comments. The directions I've provided are meant to be used only in combination with a Forest Service map and topographical maps. Keep in mind that these roads take a beating from winter storms. It is a good idea to call the Forest Service before your trip to make sure the road you plan on traveling is passable.

Many of the roads that lead to the various trailheads are very rough and/or steep, and I've denoted those trails that require low-range 4WD. As a general rule, these old logging and mining roads should not be attempted in anything other than a four-wheel-drive vehicle or two-wheel-drive truck with good ground clearance. The storms of January 1997 washed out most of the small culverts and bridges, and turned many decent 2WD roads into 4WD roads. In addition to the flood damage, many of the roads are poorly marked and overgrown. Be sure you trust your vehicle and your driving skills before you travel on these roads.

Some of the trailheads are also hard to find, and I've included detailed directions for the more difficult trails. In many cases I have listed turnoffs that should be ignored. These turnoffs are of no real importance but they are very useful as landmarks as you find your way to the trailhead.

Times in and out are approximate, of course, and are listed for a person of average fitness on a day-trip. If you plan on hiking in with a full pack for an overnight stay, add some time on both ends, especially the "time out" end. I don't want to scare anyone away from this beautiful river, but please be in good physical condition before hiking any of the trails into the Middle Fork. The steep hike downhill is hard on the knees, and the uphill climb can really tax your cardiovascular system. Needless to say, young children should not be taken on any of these trails. Most importantly, don't hike any of these trails alone. Here are some tips that will make your Middle Fork journey more enjoyable:

1. Beat the heat. In the summer, temperatures routinely reach 90+ degrees in the canyon. Start early in the morning and hike out in the evening. Be sure to carry a flashlight in case you underestimate the time required to hike out. Starting early not only makes the hike more enjoyable but it also gets you in there in time for the morning fishing. Even better, stay a day or two so you can get in plenty of morning and evening fishing.

2. Wet-wade. Leave the waders at home if you're going to hike in to the Middle Fork in the heat of summer. It's so darn hot down there you'll be ready to jump in anyway. Hike in wearing a pair of lightweight full-length pants—they'll keep the sun, bugs, and brush off your legs. When you get down to the river, trade your hiking boots for felt-soled wading shoes and jump in. The Middle Fork is a difficult stream to wade as the rocks are very slippery so be sure to bring felt-soled boots and be careful!

3. The Middle Fork is rattlesnake country. Make sure a snake-bite kit is part of your regular first-aid kit.

4. Poison oak abounds in the lower canyon. Learn how to identify it, and wear protective clothing.
5. Take lots of water and a water filter. Most of the trails cover really dry land, so you want to have a water filter to fill up your water bottles before the trip out.
6. Take a friend. This is perhaps the most important thing you can do not only to make your trip enjoyable but to make it safe. Take a camera, and you'll make memories you'll never forget.

Feather Falls Scenic Area

The 15,000-acre Feather Falls Scenic Area reaches from Lake Oroville to Milsap Bar and includes Feather Falls, Seven Falls, and portions of several tributaries. Two major tributaries, the Little North Fork and the South Branch, join the Middle Fork at Milsap Bar, contributing a major amount of water. The streambed is littered with enormous boulders, and in many places the canyon walls are sheer granite.

This grand old tree marks the beginning of the Feather Falls Trail.

As scenic as the Middle Fork is, the Scenic Area owes its name to Feather Falls, on the Fall River. The Fall River (not to be confused with the famous tributary of the Pit River) cascades over Feather Falls 640 feet into the Middle Fork arm of Lake Oroville. The sixth highest falls in the United States, Feather Falls is a very popular destination for nature lovers. Fall River is currently under consideration for Wild and Scenic River status due to its remoteness and the beauty of Feather Falls. A well-maintained four-mile trail leads to the overlook of the falls. Anglers can fish for plentiful small rainbows in the Fall River above Feather Falls.

Another scenic falls in the area is on the South Branch of the Middle Fork Feather River and is called Seven Falls (sometimes referred to as South Branch Falls). These seven stairstep waterfalls are stretched out over several miles. A very steep trail accesses these falls from the Milsap Bar Road. The trail terminates in the middle of the series of waterfalls, and it is possible to hike upstream to see two more of the falls. Like Feather Falls, this is an excellent place to take your camera. Small rainbow trout can be found in this area but the main attraction is definitely the scenery.

There are four river accesses in this area, the Dome Trail, Milsap Bar Road, and the short Crooked Bar and Cable Crossing Trails which branch off of the Milsap Bar Road. I have also included descriptions of the Seven Falls and Feather Falls trails.

Dome Trail (North Rim)

Topo Map: Brush Creek
Length: 2.0 miles
Time In: 45-60 minutes; *Time Out:* 1-2 hours
Vertical Drop: Approximately 1500 feet
> *Directions to Trailhead:* Turn off of the Oro-Quincy Highway on Bald Rock Road in the town of Brush Creek. At 2.5 miles take the turnoff to the left. At 3.7 miles the road forks—stay left. At 5.1 miles there is an intersection—follow the sign to the Dome Trail.

Comments: This is an excellent trail, well worth the effort for the view even if you don't fish. Bald Rock Dome towers over the trail, and there are magnificent views of the canyon, where barren granite slopes extend over 1,000 vertical feet down to the river's edge. The trail has numerous switchbacks to keep the gradient low, and there are even metal railings and steps on the narrow parts.

This part of the river consists of fairly large pools interspersed with whitewater. Each of these big pools is good for at least one fish. Wading is useless here since the water is too deep in between the rocks. It is difficult to move very far up- or downstream, but there is enough fishable water to make it worth the trip. The fish are larger here, with rainbows averaging fourteen to fifteen inches. Hoppers work well, as do nymphs fished deep under an indicator.

Note: I would like to point out that this trail has already been heavily damaged by people cutting switchbacks. Thousands of dollars and man-hours went into the construction of this beautiful trail. Please respect this monumental effort by sticking to the trail.

Milsap Bar Road (North/South Rim)

Directions: Turn off of the Oro-Quincy Highway onto Bald Rock Road in the town of Brush Creek. The first mile or so is paved, but the remaining eight miles is dirt and is easily traveled by 2WD vehicles. There is a good bridge at Milsap Bar, and a campground on the other side of the river. This is the only true campground on the Middle Fork. There are approximately ten campsites, a toilet, and no fee is required. You can also reach Milsap Bar from Feather Falls to the south, but this route is rougher and not as well marked. Turn off of Lumpkin Road onto Road 27 0.8 miles past the Feather Falls turnoff. Continue along this paved road for 18.2 miles, where there is a sharp turn as the road turns onto Hartman Bar Ridge. The Milsap Bar road branches off here, and the turnoff is not marked. There is, however, a small sign for the Hanson Bar Trailhead.

Comments: Milsap Bar is a very popular spot due to its close proximity to Chico and Oroville. The campground fills up on many weekends each summer. The most heavily fished part of the river, as can be expected, is in between the campground and the bridge. I like to fish from the bridge up to the Crooked Bar Trail. This is a simple matter in the fall when the water is low, but is very difficult in spring.

Since Milsap Bar is in Butte County, it is open to fishing year round. Fishing can be good into December sometimes, but winter storms often blow out the river. Nymphing is often the best bet during the winter months.

The Little North Fork and the South Branch of the Middle Fork enter the river from opposite banks at Milsap Bar. Both streams are sizable, and provide some very good fishing for the angler who is willing to hike upstream a little ways.

Crooked Bar Trail (South Rim)

Topo Map: Brush Creek
Length: 1/4 mile
Time In: 10 minutes; *Time Out:* 15 minutes
Vertical Drop: 250 feet
Directions to Trailhead: The trail starts 0.6 miles past the Milsap Bar Bridge on the south side of river. It is actually an old jeep road, although I would not recommend driving it due to its poor condition. Park at the turnoff and walk down.
Comments: Lots of good riffles, runs, and pocket water can be found here.

Cable Crossing Trail (South Rim)

Topo Map: Brush Creek
Length: 1/4 mile
Time In/Time Out: 20-30 minutes
Vertical Drop: 500 feet

Directions to Trailhead: The trail starts 1.8 miles past the Milsap Bar Bridge on the south side of the river. Milsap Bar Road is very rough where it climbs up the south side of the canyon, and 4WD is recommended.

Comments: This trail is unnamed on the map, but a cable crossing is shown over the river at the end of the trail. The cable crossing no longer exists but I had to name the trail something! The river is very rocky in this section, with deep pools and good mobility. There are a lot of good fish in this area, although they're not always willing to show themselves. The trail is in fair condition, with numerous switchbacks. The trail splits as you approach the river, with one trail going upstream and the other downstream. There is good water either way.

Seven Falls Trail (South Branch of the Middle Fork Feather River)

Topo Map: Cascade

Directions to Trailhead: Follow the directions listed for Milsap Bar Road to reach the beginning of Milsap Bar Road on the south side of the river. From here, continue 2.4 miles to the trailhead which is just before the first switchback as you head down to the river. The unmarked trail begins at a wide spot in the road. The trail is extremely steep but there are many small trees and rocks to hold on to on the way down. The trail ends in the middle of the series of waterfalls, but other trails lead upstream. This hike is very dangerous and not well-suited for children (or most adults for that matter!).

Feather Falls Trail (Fall River)

Topo Map: Brush Creek

Directions to Trailhead: Feather Falls is most easily reached from the Oro-Quincy Highway near Oroville. Punch your odometer as you turn off of the Oro-Quincy Highway onto Forbestown Road. Turn left onto Lumpkin Road at 6.1 miles. At 17.1 miles turn off of

Lumpkin Road, following the sign to the Feather Falls Trailhead. At 17.4 miles the road forks—go right. The trailhead is at 18.8 miles. All intersections are well marked.

Trailhead Facilities: There is a large parking lot at the trailhead. There are flush and vault toilets, picnic tables, and even a 5-unit campground.

Trails: About 0.3 miles from the trailhead the trail forks. The lower trail, to the left, is 3.3 miles long, and the upper trail is 4.5 miles long. Allow 1-2 hours for the lower trail and 1 1/2 to 3 hours for the upper trail. Both are excellently maintained, and offer beautiful views of Bald Rock Dome and the canyon of the Middle Fork Feather River. There are several benches along the way where you can sit down and rest. There are also many signs explaining different aspects of the local ecosystem. The lower trail drops considerably as it follows Frey Creek, and climbs steeply back up to the overlook. The upper trail is much more level. Both are quite strenuous, and are not well-suited for children. Remember, this is an eight-mile round-trip. If you're interested in fishing for some smallish rainbow trout, a trail branches off near the overlook. This trail allows access to Fall River above Feather Falls.

Comments: Feather Falls is one of the most popular attractions in the Plumas National Forest. Feather Falls cascades 640 feet down into the steep-sided canyon of the Fall River, which flows into the Middle Fork of the Feather River 1.5 miles downstream. When Lake Oroville is full, the Middle Fork backs up all the way to its confluence with Fall River, and it is possible for boaters to view the falls from the lake. From the overlook at the end of the trail you can see the entire falls. Sturdy metal railings have been installed on the trail in the steepest areas, but the potential for careless accidents still exists. Please be careful.

Hanson Bar to Butte Bar

There are four foot trails and two jeep trails that access this part of the river. As compared to the lower river, the river from Hanson Bar to Butte

A monster rainbow from Butt Valley Reservoir.

Large trout can usually be found cruising the nutrient-rich shallows of Lake Davis.

Dry Flies

Yellow Humpy   **Griffith's Gnat**   **Parachute Adams**   **Elk Hair Caddis**

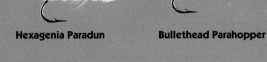

Kaufmann's Stimulator   **Hexagenia Paradun**   **Bullethead Parahopper**

Local Favorites

Rio Grande King   **Mill Creek Queen**

Royal Wulff

Yellow Palmer   **Wendell Special**

Nymphs

**Beadhead
Bird's Nest**   **Hare's Ear
Nymph**   **Pheasant Tail
Nymph**   **Prince Nymph**

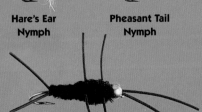

Beadhead Rubberleg Stone

LAKE FLIES

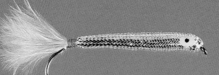

Milt's Pond Smelt

Beadhead Olive Woolly Bugger

Burnt Orange Woolly Bugger

Marabou Damsel

Simple Damsel

Blood Midge

Deep Snail

Orange Snail

Rusty Leech

This North Fork rainbow was fooled by a Royal Humpy.

The smooth, worn rocks of Grizzly Creek make it one of the most beautiful streams in the Plumas National Forest.

One of seven stair-step waterfalls at Seven Falls on the South Branch of the Middle Fork Feather River.

The New Years Floods of 1997 caused many small streams to change course. This large tree was fatally undercut and scarred, and will likely not last another season.

Many beautiful meadow streams await the hiking angler in the Plumas National Forest.

Good fish can often be found rising to midges in slow tailouts on the Middle Fork
Feather River.

Plentiful small brook trout complement the scenery at Mud Lake, near Bucks Lake.

Bar is a little smaller but still big enough to limit your mobility considerably. There are several box canyon stretches which cannot be fished without extreme difficulty. One of the most impressive box canyon areas is just upstream from the confluence of Bear Creek and the Middle Fork Feather River, and can be accessed by the Deadman Spring Trail. There are numerous mining artifacts in this area as well.

Two excellent trails, the Pacific Crest Trail and the Hartman Bar Trail, access this section of the river. The Pacific Crest Trail crosses the river via a beautiful single-arch footbridge at Butte Bar. The Hartman Bar Trail crosses the river about five miles downstream via an impressive suspension bridge. Both trails are well-maintained, well-shaded, and have a pleasant gradient.

The river fishes very well in this section. The fish average about 12 inches in length and are plentiful. Attractor dries such as Humpies and Stimulators work well, and searching nymph patterns produce when the fish won't come up. There are a lot of big pools near Hanson Bar and Hartman Bar. I have often seen fish rising to midges in the tail-outs of these pools. Indicatorless nymphing also works well at the heads of these large pools.

Hanson Bar Trail (South Rim)

Topo Map: Cascade
Length: 2 miles
Time In: 45-60 miutes; *Time Out:* 1 hour 15 minutes to 2 hours
Vertical Drop: Approximately 2300 feet
Directions to Trailhead: Turn off of Lumpkin Road onto Road 27 0.8 miles past the Feather Falls turnoff. Continue along this road for 18.2 miles, where there is a sharp turn as the road turns onto Hartman Bar Ridge. The Milsap Bar road starts here, and you will see a small sign for the Hanson Bar Trailhead. The trailhead is at the end of a two-mile dirt road which should be passable for most 2WD vehicles.
Comments: Trail is in fair condition as it follows an abandoned 4WD road. There are many switchbacks, and the trail is fairly steep.

Once you reach the river another, smaller trail leads upstream about two miles to the Graves Cabin and Kennedy Cabin. This trail is pretty narrow and passes over some very steep terrain high above the river in places. The Hanson Bar Trail is passable to horses, although the trail that goes upstream from Hanson Bar is not. There are good campsites at Hanson Bar. Although this is one of the longer trails, it accesses over two seldom-fished miles of the river. The river consists of long pools interspersed with pocket water.

Hartman Bar Trail (North/South Rim)

Topo Map: Haskins Valley
Length: 4.4 miles (north side); 4.0 miles (south side)
Time In: 1-2 hours; *Time Out:* 2-4 hours
Vertical Drop: 2800 feet north side; 2600 feet south side
Directions to North Rim Trailhead: This trailhead is well marked, and is easy to find from any of the major logging roads south of the Bucks Lake area. Most intersections will have directions to the trailhead. 4WD is recommended.
Directions to South Rim Trailhead: The Hartman Bar Trailhead is 5.1 miles east of the Milsap Bar turnoff on Hartman Bar Ridge (see directions to Milsap Bar Road). Note: The trail from the south rim is closed due to a huge washout caused by the storms of January 1997, but will hopefully be repaired soon.
Comments: This is a very popular trail as it is well maintained, shaded, and not overly steep. The only bad part is that the trail is long, although I don't really think it's as long as the signs say at the trailheads on either side. On the north side, you can refill your water bottles where the trail crosses Catrell Creek. There is a sturdy footbridge that crosses the river and is fit for horses to cross, making this one of the most popular horse trails into the Middle Fork. Below the footbridge there is some excellent fly water, a half mile of which is easily fished. An enormous pool that starts below the footbridge extends for about a quarter mile

upstream. There is some good water above this pool, but some very serious rock-climbing is necessary to access this water, as the canyon walls are quite steep. This upstream area is extremely dangerous to access, and the fishing is not really any better than in the easily accessed area below the footbridge. A bonus for the Hartman Bar Trail is that Willow Creek joins the river near the footbridge. Willow Creek is an excellent little stream, especially down by the Middle Fork where it doesn't get fished much.

Little California Jeep Trail (North Rim)

Topo Maps: Haskins Valley & Dogwood Peak

Directions: The road to the Little California Jeep Trail turns off from the Big Creek Road 2.9 miles from the T-intersection near Bucks Lake. The intersections are well-marked. Follow the signs for the Little California Trail, and take a left 6.2 miles from the Big Creek Road turnoff. The trail starts 0.7 miles farther.

Comments: This is the worst of the three jeep trails that access the Middle Fork Feather River. It's very rocky, has tight switchbacks, and shouldn't be attempted in anything but a jeep-type 4WD vehicle, trailbike, or ATV. The jeep trail stops about a 1/4 mile short of the river, and you have to hike the rest of the way. Contact the Oroville Ranger District before attempting this road. The river is very rocky here, and it's difficult to move very far up or downstream.

Stag Point Jeep Trail (South Rim)

Topo Map: Dogwood Peak

Directions: The turnoff for the Stag Point Jeep Trail is 7.9 miles east of the Hartman Bar Trailhead on Hartman Bar Ridge Road. The jeep trail can also be accessed from Little Grass Valley Reservoir. From the turnoff stay left at each fork in the road. The trailhead is 1.6 miles from the turnoff.

Comments: This road is currently closed as a result of the January 1997 storms, so contact the La Porte Ranger District for current information before making any plans. The road is very narrow and steep, with some tight switchbacks. It shouldn't be overly difficult for serious jeep enthusiasts, however.

Dead Man Spring Trail (North Rim)

Topo Map: Dogwood Peak
Length: 1/4 mile
Time In: 15 to 30 minutes; *Time Out:* 20 to 30 minutes
Vertical Drop: 800 feet
Directions to Trailhead: Turn off of Big Creek Road onto Sherman Bar Road about five miles from the T-intersection near Bucks Lake.
0.0 miles: Punch your odometer as you turnoff on the Sherman Bar Road. Go right.
7.8 miles: Ignore turnoff to the right—stay left
9.0 miles: Ignore turnoff to the right—stay left
10.5 miles: Take unmarked turnoff to the right
12.5 miles: Road forks. Park here if you wish to hike the Pacific Crest Trail, or go right 0.1 miles for the Dead Man Spring trail. There is a locked gate and private property to the left.

The last two miles is extremely steep, requiring low-range 4WD. There are two trails that start from the parking area: one to the south and one to the west. The trail to the south goes to the edge of a cliff some 200 vertical feet above the river—it is very difficult to reach the river from here. The trail to the west goes to the confluence of Bear Creek and the Middle Fork Feather River.
Comments: This is a good hike if your knees can handle it. The trail is an old skid trail used by miners to haul equipment in and out of the Middle Fork. It is very steep and covered with slippery leaves, making for a very unpleasant hike, uphill and downhill. The only good thing I can say about it is that it is short. There is only about a third of a mile of decent fly-water accessible from this trail, starting

just below Bear Creek and extending upstream. There are steep box canyons up and downstream from this stretch. Bear Creek has some good water but is also difficult to get around in.

Aside from the fishing, there are other things of interest here. There is a cable crossing at the end of the trail that leads to an old cabin on the other side of the river. There are also some old bridge pilings right below where Bear Creek enters the river. This is one of the narrowest points I've seen on the river; it must have made a nice footbridge at one time. There is also some old mining equipment on the other trail that goes southward from the parking area.

Pacific Crest Trail (North/South Rim)

Topo Map: Dogwood Peak
Length: 1 mile
Time In: 20 minutes; *Time Out:* 30 minutes
Vertical Drop: 700 feet
Directions to North Rim Trailhead: See directions for the Dead Man
   Spring Trail on page 68. Park at Dead Man Spring, where the road
   forks. The Pacific Crest Trail crosses just before the fork in the
   road. Low-range 4WD is required.
Directions to South Rim Trailhead: From the south side you can choose
   between the Pacific Crest Trailhead (2.5 miles to the river) or the
   Butte Bar Trailhead (1.5 miles to the river). The Butte Bar Trail
   joins up with the Pacific Crest Trailhead after a half mile or so.
   The road to the trailhead is very overgrown and rough on paint
   jobs. Directions are provided from the dam at Little Grass Valley
   Reservoir, near La Porte.
   0.8: Take turnoff to the left.
   2.8: Intersection—go right.
   5.4: Y, go left.
   5.7: Ignore turnoff to the left—stay to the right.
   8.0: Take turnoff to the left.
   11.3: Pacific Crest Trail crosses road.
   12.5: Butte Bar Trailhead.

Comments: This is an excellent trail and rather short if you can drive in to Deadman Spring. The river opens up a little bit here, foreshadowing the character of the river upstream. You can fish over two miles of river by hiking upstream on the north bank of the river. There is a lot of pocket water separated by small to medium-sized pools. There are plenty of campsites, and a beautiful single-arch footbridge carries the Pacific Crest Trail high over the river. Spring and early summer are the best times to connect with large fish here. You can also hike to Bear Creek from this trailhead by going the other way on the trail. It's about a 40-minute hike. There are some nice fish in this part of Bear Creek.

Cleghorn Bar to Nelson Point

This is my favorite part of the Middle Fork. Nelson Creek empties into the river at Nelson Point, changing the size and character of the river substantially. Nelson Creek is largely spring-fed so it remains high and cool year round. In the summer and fall, when the main river is getting low and warm, Nelson Creek infuses the Middle Fork with cooler water. Consequently, the river below Nelson Point is excellent from the time the runoff recedes until the end of the season in November.

The streambed is generally wide and easily negotiable in this part of the river. The rocks are smaller than in the downstream areas, and the canyon walls aren't as steep. By July the river is low enough to safely wade across, making it possible to fish long stretches of the river. This is a classic freestone riffle-run-pool type river, although there are also plenty of large pools. Since there is such a variety of water in this section, it is a good idea to come prepared with a variety of flies. Hoppers work very well from July to October. Attractor patterns like Humpies and Stimulators will work most of the time, as will searching nymph patterns. Hatches of mayflies or midges often dictate more imitative patterns, such as the Parachute Adams and Griffith's Gnat. Small Muddler Minnows are also popular.

The numbers of fish in this section are very high and there are many large fish to be had as well. Twenty-fish days are not at all uncommon.

Six foot trails and one jeep trail access this part of the river. The trails are not overly long. Two of my favorite trails, the Oddie Bar and No Ear Bar Trails, access this part of the river.

Cleghorn Bar Jeep Trail (South Rim)

Topo Maps: Onion Valley and Dogwood Peak

Directions: Drive towards La Porte on the Quincy/La Porte road 6.3 miles from the Nelson Creek Bridge, where there should be a turnoff to the right. Take this turnoff, and continue 8.2 miles to a Y, stay left. Continue 0.3 miles to the Cleghorn Bar Off Highway Vehicle (OHV) Staging Area. 4WD is required for the last four miles in to Cleghorn Bar. The road is very narrow and steep, and gets pretty rough when you get within about a mile of the river. I would recommend this road only to serious jeep enthusiasts.

Comments: This is a very popular fishing spot, but if unfamiliar with the area I suggest contacting the La Porte Ranger District for up-to-date information before driving this road. There is a rough campground with a vault toilet near the river.

Oddie Bar Trail (North Rim)

Topo Map: Onion Valley

Length: 1.3 miles

Time In: 45-60 minutes; *Time Out:* 1 1/2 to 2 1/2 hours

Vertical Drop: 1700 feet

Directions to Trailhead: Road is in good condition but new washouts due to the storms of January 1997 have turned this into a 4WD road. Turn off on a dirt road about .1 miles below Lowell Bader County Park on the east end of the town of Meadow Valley. The road sign should say "Middle Fork Trails," among other things.

0.0 miles: Turn off of Bucks Lake Road.

2.0 miles: Cross bridge over Meadow Valley Creek.

2.2 miles: Y, stay left.

5.4 miles: Deanes Valley Campground. Continue.

5.6 miles: Intersection, stay right.

5.8 miles: Y, stay left.

6.3 miles: Y, stay left.

8.0 miles: Y, go right.

8.6 miles: Follow sign that says "Middle Fork Trails, 1 1/2 miles." Stay left.

10.0 miles: Road forks and you should see the remains of an old sign. Go right for the No Ear Bar/Oddie Bar trailhead.

10.1 miles: The last .1 miles to the trailhead is very rough and requires 4WD. Stay to the right. Once you reach the trailhead, both the Oddie Bar and No Ear Bar trails continue as one for about a tenth of a mile before splitting off.

Comments: This is a good trail leading to an excellent part of the river. The trail is in fair condition and easy to follow but is a little steep. It's possible to work quite a ways up or downstream from this access. The trail is hard to locate from the river so be sure to mark the end when you get to the bottom or take a good look at your surroundings so you'll be able to find the trail on the hike out. There are many good campsites near the end of the trail.

No Ear Bar Trail (North Rim)

Topo Map: Onion Valley

Length: 1.5 miles

Time In: 45 minutes; *Time Out:* 1 to 2 hours

Vertical Drop: 1600 feet

Directions to Trailhead: See "Oddie Bar Trail" on page 71 for directions to trailhead.

Comments: This is one of my favorite Middle Fork Trails for a variety of reasons. The road to the trailhead is pretty good, and the trail itself is in good condition, although it is a bit steep. It is rather short, however, and it leads to some of the best fly-water the Middle Fork has to offer. It is easy to work your way up- and downstream from this access.

Minerva Bar Trail (South Rim)

Topo Map: Onion Valley

Length: 1 mile

Time In: 40-60 minutes; *Time Out:* 1 to 1.5 hours

Vertical Drop: Approximately 1400 feet

Directions to Trailhead: This trail can be reached from Quincy by driving towards La Porte on the Quincy-La Porte Road.

0.0 miles: Punch your odometer as you cross the Nelson Creek Bridge.

5.0 miles: Take turnoff to the right (road 37).

6.1 miles: Turn off to the right on the Belfrin Mine Road, which is marked by a blank sign.

7.9 miles: Road forks, go left.

8.0 miles: There is an intersection here. Stay left. Within about 100 yards you will see another blank sign. Continue on to the right. The road gets very steep here and low-range 4WD is recommended.

8.7 miles: Road forks, go left.

8.9 miles: Clearing. Park here. The trail goes down to the west.

Comments: This part of the river is fairly easy to move around in, especially when the water levels drop in the summer. You can travel very far upstream or downstream. The trail is easy to follow in most places but is very steep. There are several places where the trail forks. If you take the most heavily traveled trail you will stay to the right and actually reach the river upstream from Minerva Bar. This trail is so steep near the bottom that someone has tied ropes to the trees to make for an easier climb. To avoid the ropes you must leave the trail and head westward before the trail contours to the east. Definitely take an Onion Valley topo map along on this hike.

Hottentot Trail (South Rim)

Topo Maps: Onion Valley, Blue Nose Mountain

Length: 1 mile

Time In: 30 minutes; *Time Out:* 45-60 minutes

Vertical Drop: Approximately 900 feet

Directions to Trailhead: The road to trailhead can be reached by driving 1.5 miles past the Nelson Creek Bridge towards La Porte on the Quincy-La Porte Road. Turn right on this unmarked 4WD road and continue another 1.5 miles to a clearing. Park here; the remaining 0.2 miles to the trailhead is too narrow to drive. The trail starts at the end of this road, and is very obvious.

Comments: This is one of my favorite trails. It's short and leads to some great water. Like most of the other trails, this is another short but steep one. The gold miners who built all these trails were obviously more interested in mining than in trail construction, and I can't say that I blame them! The river is excellent here, consisting of small to medium pools and a lot of pocket water. By crossing the river you can get down as far as Bachs Creek, about a mile downstream. There is also good mobility in the upstream direction.

Lost Cabin Spring Trail (North Rim)

Topo Maps: Onion Valley, Blue Nose Mountain

Length: 0.8 miles

Time In: 40 minutes; *Time Out:* One hour

Vertical Drop: 800 feet

Directions to Trailhead: This is a definite 4WD road, with the last quarter mile requiring low-range 4WD due to steepness. It's also very overgrown so don't take a nice vehicle down there. There is only one tough spot, a narrow washout within a stone's throw of the end of the road. To get to the trailhead, drive 6.7 miles down the Quincy-La Porte Road from Quincy. There will be a turnoff to the right (23N92) marked Lost Cabin Spring and Middle Fork Trails. Continue down this road for approximately two miles where you will reach a Y, and go left. Stay left. Lost Cabin Spring is a little over a mile down this road, which is very overgrown. Park at the small clearing at the end of the road. The trail starts on the west side of the clearing and follows a contour to the west for

about a hundred yards before splitting into two trails. The Lost
Cabin Spring Trail branches off to the left, going down the
mountainside. The other trail, which continues along the side of
the mountain, goes to Bachs Creek.

Comments: This trail is good for evening fishing since you can get out
relatively quickly and easily. The trail is very steep, though, and
it's easy to miss some of the switchbacks. There are a couple spots,
especially down close to the water, where some very basic rock-
climbing skills are required. There isn't much pocket water in this
stretch. There are a lot of deep pools and runs that are well-suited
to deep indicator nymphing and sinking-line fishing.

Nelson Point Trail (South Rim)

Topo Map: Blue Nose Mountain
Length: 1/4 mile
Time In/Time Out: 15-20 minutes
Directions to Trailhead: From Quincy on the Quincy-La Porte Road,
drive 1.0 miles past the bridge over the Middle Fork. Take the
turnoff to your right, and drive to the end of the road. There is a
California Department of Fish and Game catch-report card box at
the beginning of the trail.

Comments: The quarter-mile Nelson Point Trail is just one of many trails
that used to lead to the rip-roaring mining camp called Nelson
Point. Nelson Point prospered from 1850 until the early 1900s. In
the early years the town was home to some very rough characters,
and was dubbed "The wickedest town in California." Although
primarily a mining community, hotels, stores, and saloons sprang
up to entice travelers along the Quincy-La Porte wagon road,
completed in 1866. Not a single structure remains at Nelson Point
today, making it hard to imagine all the activity that once took
place there. The absence of structures is common at many historic
sites because the lumber was scavenged to use in other places.

The Nelson Point Trail leads down to the confluence of
Nelson Creek and the Middle Fork Feather River. This is a good

way to get down to the river early in the season, but the high water makes it difficult to fish upstream or downstream. Later in the season, you can work your way up or down quite a ways. This is one of the shortest and most popular access trails to the Middle Fork, and the fishing suffers accordingly. However, there is plenty of good water to fish from here, and many good fish are caught in this stretch each year.

Nelson Point to Graeagle

The Middle Fork Feather River is obviously smaller above its confluence with Nelson Creek. The character of the river also changes drastically throughout this section. Near Nelson Point and the Quincy-La Porte Road Bridge, the Middle Fork retains the rocky, rugged characteristic of the lower canyon. Fells Flat Road and the Buckhorn Mine trail access this part of the river. As you follow the river upstream, the canyon opens up and the gradient of the stream decreases considerably. Accessing the river is easy as the river flows past the towns of Gracagle, Cromberg, and Sloat. You can fish the river by hiking the railroad tracks, which emerge from the Spring Garden Tunnel just downstream from the town of Sloat. Numerous maintenance roads offer access to the railroad and the river in this area. The river is very good near Two Rivers and Camp Layman. Catchable rainbows are stocked in the part of the river that flows through the Feather River Park near Graeagle, and wild rainbows are plentiful throughout the river.

The best time to fish this part of the river is before August. June is a great month. By the end of July, though, the river is too warm and the fish only feed in the very early and late hours. Even in the early months, the best time to be on the river is the evening. The surface action doesn't start until about seven p.m., and reaches a peak about an hour before dark. Caddisflies, aquatic moths, and creamy mayflies hatch profusely in June and early July. The fish feed heavily on midges throughout the season. The river is lined with grassy banks in this section, so watch for fish rising under the overhanging leaves.

Quincy-La Porte Road Bridge

The Quincy-La Porte Road Bridge crosses the river a mile upstream from Nelson Point. There are rough campsites with vault toilets on both sides of the bridge. There is a really nice pool right below the bridge, and good water both up- and downstream. This is a popular place to fish given its close proximity to Quincy. As the area right around the bridge can get fished out by the end of the season, it is often beneficial to hike up- or downstream a little ways.

Fells Flat Road (North Rim)

Topo Maps: Spring Garden, Blue Nose Mountain
Directions: From Quincy, drive 5.7 miles down the Quincy-La Porte
   Road and turn off on road 23N22, which should be marked for
   Fells Flat. Continue down this road and turn off on road 23N22F,
   which goes down to the river.
Comments: This one gets fished quite a bit but still produces. There is
   good water downstream.

Buckhorn Mine Trail (North Rim)

Topo Map: Blue Nose Mountain
Directions: Same as for Fells Flat, but take turnoff 23N22A instead of
   turnoff 23N22F. This 4WD road is rather narrow—watch out for
   rocks hidden by brush on the side of the road. The trail branches
   off from a wide spot in the road and is fairly obvious.
Comments: The trail is short but steep, perhaps a 1/4 mile long.

Above Graeagle

The river gets pretty low and warm above Graeagle but there are still fish to be had. One would be wise to fish early and late in the day, and to avoid the slow water. Spring is the best time for the uppermost part of the river. The river is good in and around Clio. Concentrate on the faster, more oxygenated parts of the river.

Tributaries to the Middle Fork Feather River

Among the tributaries to the Middle Fork are some of the best small streams in the Plumas National Forest. They are rough little streams full of hardy rainbow and brown trout. Some of these fish have topped the five-pound mark, and many will reach a foot in length. Most, however, are pan-sized at best. These little fish test your reflexes with their quick strikes. If you set the hook too hard they'll often fly out of the water and smack you

Countless miles of delightful small streams wind
through the Plumas National Forest.

in the face. The paradox of fishing small streams is that you have to set the hook hard and fast to hook the small fish but that same motion will break off your fly if it's taken by a large fish. After catching a lifetime's worth of fingerlings and breaking off too many nice fish, I'm training myself to set the hook slowly and firmly, as if every strike was a large fish.

Trout in small streams are very opportunistic. Since the fish will strike most anything, you might as well fish with a fly you can see. Big bucktail and hair-wing flies are popular for fishing the small streams.

Ladybugs can be found in abundance along the banks of the small streams of the Plumas National Forest, and are an important source of food for the trout.

The bigger flies float well, are easy to see, and have a tendency to weed out the smaller fish. One of my favorite small-stream flies is the Yellow Palmer. It is very simple to tie, which is important when fishing small streams where more flies are lost in trees. Medium to large stonefly nymphs work well in the early season also.

The only intense "hatch" I've ever seen on these small streams is the ladybug hatch. They seem to hatch periodically throughout the summer and fall. Oftentimes ladybugs can be found by the thousands on logs and trees near the smaller streams. Sometimes they're so thick that you don't see them at first. Many of them make their way into the water and are eaten by trout. I've caught trout during ladybug hatches that were so gorged with the bugs that their stomachs felt crunchy. Don't worry about exact imitations for ladybugs. I've found that when the fish are feasting on ladybugs they aren't very selective.

South Branch of the Middle Fork Feather River

The South Branch flows into the Middle Fork just below the campground at Milsap Bar. It gets fished pretty hard near the campground but is good if you hike upstream a little ways. You can only hike a couple miles before reaching the impassable Seven Falls, which are detailed in the section about the Feather Falls Scenic Area. The Seven Falls Trail terminates in the middle of the falls but the fishing isn't especially good there. The South Branch is much better upstream near the town of Cascade.

Little North Fork of the Middle Fork Feather River

The Little North Fork is one of the larger tributaries to the Middle Fork Feather River. Through an extensive network of tributaries it drains the region south of Bucks Lake. Many of the tributaries to the Little North Fork are most easily accessible from the Bucks Lake Area. The Little North Fork is accessible at Milsap Bar where it flows into the Middle Fork Feather River. Like the South Branch, the Little North Fork suffers from angling pressure near Milsap Bar, and improves dramatically upstream. The next road access is just below the Little North Fork campground. The stream is good here but again suffers from over-fishing. Actually, it suffers from over-killing. If everyone practiced catch and release this would be an excellent stream.

Many of the tributaries to the Little North Fork are excellent. Although parts of these creeks can be accessed along the roadside, better fishing can be found by hiking into the more remote areas. The same goes for the Little North Fork itself. There are miles and miles of water that are only accessible on foot. These small streams produce some very good fish for the angler who goes to the trouble of hiking into the more remote segments.

If you're in this area you should definitely check out Robinson Mine on Frasier Creek. There is an impressive stamp mill on the east side of the creek. This mining operation peaked more recently than most of the mines in the area, remaining active well into the 1900s. The unrestored Robinson Mine stamp mill rivals the one on display at the Plumas-Eureka State Park in the Lakes Basin.

The Little North Fork watershed provides excellent small-stream fly fishing.

Willow Creek, tributary to the Middle Fork Feather River.

Willow Creek

Willow Creek is a fine stream, especially down near its confluence with the Middle Fork Feather River. You can fish the lower part of the creek from the bottom of the Hartman Bar Trail. On several trips to Hartman Bar I have caught more and larger fish out of Willow Creek than the Middle Fork. There is a mixed bag of rainbows and browns in Willow Creek. The browns are more common in the upper part of the creek, which can be accessed via dirt roads south of Bucks Lake. Be warned that Willow Creek gets its name rightly, and the upper half of the creek is very difficult to fish.

Bear Creek is one of the prettiest tributaries to the Middle Fork Feather River.

Bear Creek

Bear Creek is an excellent hike-in destination. Although logging roads cross it in the headwaters, the creek is quite small up there. To get to the best fishing, you'll have to fish farther downstream. The Pacific Crest Trail crosses Bear Creek about a mile upstream from its confluence with the Middle Fork Feather River. Good fish can be caught in this part of the creek. Small fish abound upstream. On a recent day-trip into upper Bear Creek a friend and I caught well over a hundred fish between us. This is the kind of fishing CalTrout recently referred to as "fast-action" fishing. It's kind of like the way T-ball can be a lot more fun to watch than professional baseball. Don't be afraid to keep a limit of these small fish. It will reduce the competition and the fish will grow larger. Keep the smallest fish and release the larger ones.

Nelson Creek

Nelson Creek is one of the finest small streams in the Plumas National Forest. This beautiful stream is under consideration for Wild & Scenic River status. The best part of the creek is from Nelson Point to the Quincy-La Porte Road bridge over the creek. For its size, this stream produces some very large trout. Average fish are ten to twelve inches, and fish up to fifteen inches long are not uncommon. Unfortunately, most of these larger fish end up in the frying pan early in the season. Many good fish also move up from the Middle Fork to seek relief from increasing water temperatures in the summer. Attractor dries work well, although the fish seem to favor caddis patterns and Stimulators. A pair of hip boots are all you need to wade this shallow stream.

The best way to access the creek is via the Nelson Point Trail. Fish upstream, but please be aware that the next place to hike out is at the bridge two miles upstream. Two miles doesn't sound like much, but that's a lot of water to fish in one day. Remember to allow enough time to hike back downstream to the trail before dark.

The Upper Feather River Lakes

The California State Water Project was conceived to transport surplus water from the Feather River watershed and Sacramento-San Joaquin River Delta to areas of need in the San Francisco Bay Area, the San Joaquin Valley, and Southern California. The Upper Feather River lakes, Lake Davis, Frenchman Lake, and Antelope Lake, were constructed in the 1960s as the cornerstone of this grand project, which has grown to include 18 reservoirs, 17 pumping plants, eight hydroelectric power plants, and 550 miles of aqueducts and pipelines. The Upper Feather River project initially consisted of five reservoirs; Abby Bridge and Dixie Refuge Reservoirs were never constructed.

The three Upper Feather River lakes are true multi-purpose reservoirs. In addition to storing water that will eventually be collected downstream at Lake Oroville, these reservoirs provide diverse recreational opportunities, including water skiing, swimming, sailing, camping, and fishing. Excellent camping, fishing access, boat launching, and day-use facilities exist at all three lakes. There are over 500 campsites distributed between the numerous campgrounds at Lake Davis, Frenchman Lake, and Antelope Lake.

Fishing is the most popular recreational activity at the Upper Feather River lakes. The lakes are relatively shallow and are able to support abundant aquatic vegetation. The aquatic vegetation supports aquatic invertebrates, which in turn are eaten by trout. All three lakes host impressive damselfly hatches. Supporting little natural reproduction, the three lakes are stocked regularly with catchable rainbow trout. Thousands of fingerling rainbows are planted as well. The lakes are also home to catfish and bass, and many varieties of rough fish.

In addition to excellent lake fishing, the three Upper Feather River lakes also offer fine tailwater streams. The improvement of down-stream fish habitat was one of the major concerns in the construction of the reservoirs. Tailwater streams support good populations of trout because they have a constant flow of water. Free-flowing tributaries and water coming over the spillway often increase the flow, but tailwaters rarely get lower than the state-mandated flow. In any case, the fish have a very stable environment in which to live. The fisheries of Indian, Big Grizzly, and Little Last Chance creeks have been improved dramatically by the construction of the Upper Feather River lakes.

Lake Davis (5775 feet)

Lake Davis is a true trophy-trout destination. A favorite spot for float-tubers from Reno, the Bay Area, Sacramento, and everywhere in between, Lake Davis produces more large trout each year than any other body of water in the Plumas National Forest. Completed in 1966, Lake Davis is also the largest of the three Upper Feather River lakes, storing a maximum of 84,370 acre-feet of water.

Trout fishing is a year-round event at Lake Davis. The road to the lake is plowed during the winter, but the road around the lake is often snowbound until May or June. Ice fishing is popular in the winter months. Float-tubers descend upon the lake after ice-out in the spring.

During June and July the shoreline vegetation of Lake Davis is adorned with multitudes of damselfly shucks.

Until the snow melts on the road going around the lake, float-tube access is limited to Catfish Cove on the southern tip of the lake, although boaters can put in at the Honker Cove boat ramp.

The shallow coves on the west side of the lake are the prime spots for fly fishing. These shallow, weedy areas pump out the majority of the aquatic insects that provide nourishment for the trout. There are six roads that branch off the main road which access the west side of the lake. From south to north, they are Eagle Point, Old Camp 5 Boat Ramp, Jenkins Point, Road 24N71Y (aka Fugawe Point), Cow Creek, and Freeman Creek. Some of these roads have gates to contain the cattle that graze in the area. Be sure to close these gates behind you. The east side of the lake is also good. The main channel through the lake is closest to the east bank, so deeper water can be accessed from that side. It is often rather windy at Lake Davis, and the wind direction may be a factor in choosing which side of the lake to fish.

Large rainbows can be found cruising the coves and inlets during April and May. The fish are only about two to six feet below the surface this time of year. Woolly Buggers, streamers, and large Pheasant Tail or Bird's Nest nymphs produce well when trolled or retrieved slowly. As the weather and water temperatures warm, *Callibaetis* mayflies start to hatch dependably. *Callibaetis* nymph imitations can be deadly when fished under an indicator this time of year. Dark tan nymphs with black tails and wingcases work well in sizes 14-16. *Callibaetis* emergers also work when fished right in the surface film. Blood midge pupae imitations also produce well this time of year. The blood midges hatch several times throughout the year, and it is a good idea to have some blood midge pupae imitations on hand when at Davis. *Callibaetis* hatches, streamers, and blood midges provide the main action until the beginning of the damselfly hatch in mid-June.

Once the damselfly hatch gets under way, most everything else is forgotten. Damselflies begin their migration from the weed beds to the shoreline mid-May and the hatch reaches peak intensity in mid-June. The damselflies are active throughout the month of June, and begin to thin out by the middle of July. The damselfly hatch attracts the attention of some very large fish at Lake Davis. Fish caught during the damselfly hatch average eighteen to twenty inches in length. These large fish cruise the shallows, intercepting the nymphs as they swim towards shore.

There are dozens of damselfly patterns that will successfully imitate the damsel nymphs at Lake Davis. The key is to have several different patterns on hand, tied in different sizes and colors. The damsel nymphs can range from fluorescent green to olive to a dullish brown in color, and can vary considerably in size. The fish become selective to a certain size and color, and if you don't have it, you're often out of luck. I have had the most success with the No-Name Damsel, Burk's Damsel, and simple damsel patterns of my own design. The Sheep Creek Special is a popular damsel imitation at Davis as well. Be careful when buying commercial damsel patterns because nearly all of them are tied too large. It's a good idea to tie up some smaller versions of the standard patterns, and plenty of them. Another important factor is the speed of your retrieve. Take a few minutes to observe the nymphs in the water. They can swim fast, but only when they're chasing something, such as your float tube. Most of the time they move very slowly. Adjust your retrieve accordingly.

Although float tubing offers more versatility, wading can be very productive when the fish are feeding close to shore. Sight-casting is often possible, and is facilitated by a higher fishing platform such as a boat or pram. When no risers are within casting range, fish near weed beds and other structure. Many fish cruise in somewhat regular patterns, and will be seen rising periodically in the same spot. It is also a good idea to have some adult damselfly imitations on hand in case the wind comes up. When gusts of wind blow across the lake, fish hold just down-wind from emergent weeds, waiting for the nymphs and adults to be blown into the water. The fish tend to rise more violently to the fallen adult damselflies, since they are likely to escape.

The end of the damselfly hatch in late July often coincides with increasing water temperatures. Fly fishing becomes difficult as the fish move into deeper water. Woolly Buggers and other leech patterns work well when fished in deep water on a fast-sinking line. The fishing often doesn't improve much until mid-September. As the water cools, fish move back into the shallows and become more accessible to the fly-fisher. Blood midge hatches often provide some action in September. Big fish start showing up as October rolls around. Three- to six-pounders are very common in the fall. Streamers, such as Matukas, Muddler Minnows, Zonkers, and leech patterns, work well at this time. Fish also move into the shallows in search of snails this time of year. Lake Davis has a large population of aquatic snails. The trout love these snails and effective snail patterns can catch large fish. The typical snail pattern is a truncated Crystal Bugger, size 10 or 12, in brown, orange, or olive. They can be fished under an indicator or retrieved slowly. Snail patterns work year round at Lake Davis, and the trout often become very selective to them.

There are three campgrounds at Lake Davis: Lightning Tree, Grasshopper Flat, and Grizzly. There are three paved boat ramps and numerous places to launch car-top boats. Two roads access Lake Davis from Highway 70 near Portola. Lake Davis is only fifty miles from Reno. The fly shops listed in Appendix C usually have up-to-date information on Lake Davis.

Pike Eradication at Lake Davis

Northern pike were discovered in Lake Davis in 1994, three years after they were successfully eradicated from Frenchman Lake in 1991. To prevent the pike from washing out of the lake and establishing populations elsewhere, the California Department of Fish & Game poisoned Lake Davis in October 1997. The lake took much longer to detoxify than was planned, and the lake was not reopened and stocked with fish until July 1998. Over a million trout, mostly fingerlings, were planted by the end of the season. Lacking competition from other species, these fingerlings should grow very fast. Despite the poisoning and lack of fish, Lake Davis had an excellent damselfly hatch in 1998. The aquatic snails are also highly abundant. The holdover catchable and trophy-sized trout should provide plenty of action in 1999 and the lake should be excellent again by the year 2000.

Big Grizzly Creek

A healthy amount of water is released into Big Grizzly Creek from Lake Davis, resulting in some good trout habitat. Although the creek is a little fast, fish can be found holding against undercut banks and behind other types of structure. The best place to access the creek is from the access road near the dam. The first two pools below the dam can be good, but it is often worthwhile to hike downstream and fish back up to the dam.

Frenchman Lake (5588 feet)

Frenchman Lake was the first reservoir of the Upper Feather River Project to be completed. In 1961 it began to fill, and Frenchman Lake quickly gained a reputation as one of the most outstanding fishing lakes in California. Although the fishery of every reservoir declines after it hits its peak, Frenchman Lake has found a healthy equilibrium. Similar to Lake Davis, Frenchman Lake is relatively shallow, with much aquatic growth. The shallow areas are like cafeterias for the fish, where they can find all kinds of nourishment, including mayflies, midges, damselflies, dragonflies, and all sorts of other goodies. The only thing that drives the

Frenchman Lake is a popular spot for migrating waterfowl as well as fly fishers.

fish away from the shallows is temperature. By mid-July or August water temperatures are often high enough to force the fish into the depths. The deepest water is near the dam, and large flies trolled on full-sink lines can be very effective in this area.

Woolly Bugger derivatives are very popular at Frenchman Lake. Fly-tiers often add shiny materials like sparkle chenille, Krystal Flash, and Flashabou to liven up their patterns. These large patterns work well when trolled over shallow weed beds in the spring and fall. In summer, when the fish have retreated to the depths, troll these patterns on a sinking line. Small Crystal Buggers also work well as snail imitations.

The shallow coves on the west side of the lake are great for wading. Fish work these coves in the morning and evening hours. *Callibaetis* mayfly, blood midge, and damselfly hatches coincide with hatches at Lake Davis. In the fall, switch from insect patterns to streamers. Zonkers, Woolly Buggers, Matukas, and leech patterns work well on a moderate to fast retrieve. Many large trout are hooked on streamers in the fall.

Frenchman Lake is dominated by rainbow trout. The trout have grown quickly since the lake was poisoned in 1991 to eradicate illegally introduced northern pike. The lake was stocked with fingerling Eagle Lake trout, and lacking competition from other species such as sunfish, pike, and bass, the trout have done very well. Fish in the 20-inch range are becoming commonplace, and electro-shocking surveys confirm the fact that the lake is full of big trout. Having fallen under the shadow of nearby Lake Davis in recent years, the fishing action at Frenchman Lake seems to be more consistent than at Davis. Only forty miles from Reno, Frenchman Lake is rapidly gaining in popularity.

Although you can park your car and fish from any point on the lake, there are six official Fishing Access points. Starting on the west side of the lake and moving clockwise, they are Lunker Point, Snallygaster Point, Nightcrawler Bay, Salmon Egg Shoal, Turkey Point, and Crystal Point. Each access has a vault toilet. There are also five campgrounds to choose from at Frenchman Lake. Big Cove, Spring Creek, and Frenchman campgrounds are right on the lake, while the Chilcoot and Cottonwood Springs campgrounds are only a short distance away. Paved boat ramps can be found at Lunker Point and Frenchman Campground.

Little Last Chance Creek

Frenchman Lake usually fills up and spills over after average winters, spilling a good number of large trout into Little Last Chance Creek. Although large concentrations of these bruisers will be found right below the dam, some fish end up several miles downstream. This wash-out phenomenon is no secret, and Little Last Chance Creek is one of the premiere Opening Day destinations in the Plumas National Forest. The high Opening Day flows make fly fishing difficult, but it can be done.

Even if you miss out on the Opening Day action, there is good fly fishing to be had in the creek throughout the season. A constant flow is released from Frenchman Reservoir all summer long, which fosters a healthy population of brown trout. These fish average ten to twelve inches in length, and provide fine sport for dry-fly enthusiasts on summer evenings. Little Last Chance Creek has a pretty swift current, and overhanging limbs and streamside brush provide interesting casting challenges.

Little Last Chance Creek, below Frenchman Lake, is home to a healthy population of brown trout.

The canyon of Little Last Chance Creek below Frenchman Lake.

Antelope Lake (5002 feet)

Antelope Lake is tucked away in one of the more remote parts of the Plumas National Forest. Although it contributes a significant amount of water to the State Water Project, Antelope Lake was created primarily for recreational purposes. Among the various recreational opportunities that exist at the lake, fishing is the most popular. Three fishing access points, Guiney Point, Lunker Landing, and Eagle Lookout, provide shore-fishing access, and boat fishing is popular as well.

Like most reservoirs, the fishing in Antelope Lake hit a peak several years after it was filled and has continually declined. Although it is a very productive lake, like the two other Upper Feather River lakes, the major problem at Antelope Lake is competition with introduced warmwater species such as panfish, bullheads, bass, and other rough fish. Antelope Lake was poisoned several times to remove these fish, and the trout fishery improved dramatically until the warmwater fish regained their foothold. Public sentiment now effectively prohibits the

Department of Fish and Game from managing lakes through the application of rotenone. Consequently, the warmwater fish dominate the lake and the majority of the trout action results from annual stockings of catchable rainbows and brookies.

Concentrate your angling efforts on inlet areas and submerged streambeds at Antelope Lake. It is difficult to fly-fish from shore here as a wall of aquatic vegetation rings the shoreline of the lake. A float tube or boat will get you out beyond this band of vegetation. Sink-tip and full-sink lines usually work best. Fly selections should be heavy on Woolly Bugger and damselfly nymph patterns. Antelope Lake has a decent damselfly hatch that coincides with the hatch at Lake Davis. It's not nearly as intense at Antelope Lake, but it still attracts a lot of attention from the trout.

In addition to the three official fishing access points, anglers can fish from the campgrounds and day-use areas. The dam is also a popular spot. Boats can be launched at the Lost Cove boat ramp on the north side of the lake. Antelope Lake is most easily reached from Taylorsville.

Indian Creek

Indian Creek is one of the better small streams in the Plumas National Forest. Although this is not the typical crystal-clear mountain stream, it's full of wild brown trout and the silty water actually makes it easy to stalk the fish. Indian Creek is best above Genesee Valley, where it is easily accessible along the road between Taylorsville and Antelope Lake. There are numerous pull-outs where you can park and walk right down to the water. There are well over five miles of creek along the roadside. The best time to fish Indian Creek is in the spring as soon as Antelope Lake has stopped spilling over, or is just barely spilling over. If a lot of water is going over the spillway, Indian Creek is difficult to fly-fish. Searching nymph patterns work well when the fish aren't rising. Indian Creek is not very deep so be careful not to get hung up on the bottom. Hatches of yellow stones, tan caddisflies, and pale morning duns usually come off on summer evenings. The fish aren't overly selective, though. My usual strategy at Indian Creek is to fish nymphs until the fish start to strike at my indicator. The last three hours of daylight are the prime time to fish here.

Taylor Lake (6803 feet)

This lake has a reputation for sizable brook trout. Just the right size for float-tubing, it also has a makeshift launch ramp for aluminum boats, although I wouldn't want to haul a trailer up there. Situated about five miles west of Antelope Lake (as the crow flies), this lake is really in the middle of nowhere. 4WD is recommended for this road. This is a fairly deep lake, especially in the spring. There is an outlet that allows the lake to be drained about six feet or so throughout the summer. There are plenty of weeds in the shallows to harbor food for the brook trout. Fingerling brookies are stocked annually at Taylor Lake. They grow large in this food-rich environment, sometimes past the sixteen-inch mark. Sink-tip lines are in order when the lake is high, but a floating line is all you need later in the year. Cast Olive Beadhead Woolly Buggers, damsel patterns, and golden Flash Tail streamers.

Crystal Lake (6689 feet)

Tucked up against the steep northeast side of Mt. Hough (pronounced Huff), Crystal Lake provides some good fishing for smallish brookies and the occasional brown. It is possible to fish this lake from shore since you can walk around the lake, but a float tube is much better. Be sure to visit Mt. Hough Lookout while you're there. There is a great view, and the lookout itself is rather impressive.

South Fork of the Feather River

The South Fork is by far the smallest of the three forks of the Feather River that flow through the Plumas National Forest. Like the North Fork, the South Fork used to be an excellent stream before it was dammed from top to bottom. Small rainbows are now the main attraction at the South Fork, but some larger fish can be caught in the section immediately below Little Grass Valley Reservoir. The South Fork area can be reached most easily from Oroville, or via the gravel Quincy-La Porte Road from Quincy. La Porte is the largest town in the area. There are campgrounds at Little Grass Valley Reservoir and Sly Creek Reservoir.

Some of the better places to access the river are at the dam on Little Grass Valley Reservoir, the South Fork Diversion Dam, and Golden Trout Crossing. The South Fork Diversion Dam is accessible from Mooreville Ridge via road 21N11Y. Downstream, Golden Trout Crossing offers good access to the river but don't get your hopes up; there are no golden trout to be found here. The South Fork is a very clear stream so stalk carefully and fish in the morning and evenings.

Little Grass Valley Reservoir (5034 feet)

Little Grass Valley Reservoir can be found near La Porte. It is a popular lake for people who like to troll for kokanee and trout, but fly-fishers can also do well here. The main action is on stocked rainbows and the occasional brown trout. The most productive areas to fish are the points and tributary inlets. Spring and fall are the best times, as the trout are feeding near the surface. During the summer, trout can be found feeding in the shallows in the morning and evening hours. Midges often hatch profusely on summer evenings, and can be imitated with small Brassies, Griffith's Gnats, and Blood Midge Pupae.

There are six campgrounds at Little Grass Valley Reservoir, offering nearly three-hundred campsites. Nearby La Porte is one of the oldest towns in Plumas County. La Porte is often referred to as the birth-place of competitive skiing. The world's first ski club was organized in 1866 at La Porte. Although the nearby Plumas-Eureka Mine in the Lakes Basin holds the honor of having the world's first mechanized ski lift, La Porte can lay claim to the world's first downhill ski race. The competitors skied on long, Norwegian-style snowshoes. Skiing, snowshoeing, and snowmobiling are still very popular winter sports in this area, and throughout the Plumas National Forest.

Sly Creek (3530 feet) and
Lost Creek Reservoirs (3275 feet)

These steep-banked, turquoise reservoirs are not very conducive to shore-fishing, but trout can be caught from boat or float tube. Sly Creek

Reservoir is drained rather drastically throughout the season, but the launch ramp is functional even when the water is low. There are two campgrounds at Sly Creek Reservoir. Upstream from Sly Creek Reservoir, Lost Creek provides some good fly fishing. Lost Creek is also good below Lost Creek Reservoir, as fish wash out of the reservoir into the creek in the spring.

Lakes Basin

First-time visitors to the Lakes Basin are faced with a tough decision: Where should I go and what should I do during my short stay?! There are so many trails to hike and lakes to fish that even a long stay in the area will never seem long enough. In addition to dozens of trout-bearing lakes and streams, there are numerous waterfalls, the Plumas-Eureka State Park, and countless trails, all of which interconnect with the Pacific Crest Trail. With all these different things to see and do, most visitors make this area an annual destination.

During your travels through the lakes basin you are likely to notice many shallow ponds, marshes, and meadows. These grassy depressions offer an excellent lesson in geology. Lakes, like humans, trout, and mayflies, have a life cycle. Beginning as relatively deep, lifeless tarns, lakes gradually fill up with silt and turn into shallow, rich lakes. Rich, shallow lakes can support more biomass than deep lakes; keep this fact in mind when you fish the lakes in the area. As the lake continues to fill it turns into a marsh, then a meadow. In the Lakes Basin you can see examples of every stage in a lake's life cycle. There are deep tarns, shallow lakes, marshes, seasonal ponds, and meadows. Keep your eyes open for these sights, as well as beautiful wildflowers and birds, lofty peaks, and cascading waterfalls.

Gold Lake (not to be confused with the tiny Gold Lake near Bucks Lake) is the largest lake in the area, and holds the largest fish by far. It is a fairly large lake considering its high elevation. Like the other lakes in the area, Gold Lake stays nice and cool all summer long. Gold Lake is also over 100 feet deep and is able to support a healthy population of mackinaw, or lake trout. Planted annually with mackinaw fingerlings,

Gold Lake is turning into one of the best mackinaw lakes in the state of California. Large browns are very common as well, and catchable rainbows and brookies have been planted in recent years.

Long Lake is the second largest lake in the area, and like most of the lakes, it is only accessible by trail. There are a great number of trails in the Lakes Basin, all of which are well-marked, and the trailheads are easy to find. All of the trails interconnect with each other and with the Pacific Crest Trail, which rides high atop the ridge overlooking the Lakes Basin. You can drive on a paved road up to Packer Saddle and the Pacific Crest Trail from the Sardine Lakes turnoff. From Packer Saddle you can hike to the Sierra Buttes Lookout, Deer Lake, Summit Lake, Tamarack Lakes, or Little Deer Lake. The Sierra Buttes Lookout, at 8591 feet, offers an astounding view of the southern end of the Lakes Basin. Other popular trails include the Frazier Falls Trail, Round Lake Loop, Long Lake Trail, and Jamison Lake Trail.

Fly fishing is generally good in the lakes in the area. The high elevation of the area ensures that water temperatures remain comfortable for the trout all summer long. The downside is that the area remains snowbound well into May, and sometimes even June and July. You can expect to be able to hike into and fish most of the lakes by late June, although late-spring snows can sometimes delay things a bit. Fishing can be very good when the lakes ice-out in May and June, although it is difficult to get to most of the lakes at that time. Some of the better fishing lakes in the Lakes Basin include Gold Lake, Long Lake, Smith Lake, Lower and Upper Salmon lakes, Packer Lake, Lower and Upper Sardine lakes, Tamarack Lakes, and Grass, Rock, Wades, and Jamison lakes. Although the Lakes Basin is known best for its lake fishing, there are also several small streams in the area. Graeagle Creek, Frazier Creek, and Salmon Creek are full of eager little rainbows and browns, and the North Fork of the Yuba River is nearby as well.

Most of the lakes in the Lakes Basin have been stocked by truck, plane, or milk can at some time in their history. Gold Lake, Lower Sardine Lake, and Packer Lake are frequently stocked by truck with catchable rainbows and brook trout. Many of the remote lakes cannot support wild populations of trout. Some of them are subject to occasional winterkill. Some of the lakes that can support wild populations can only support brook trout, which have a tendency to overpopulate and become stunted. To combat these problems, the California Department of Fish and Game stocks the remote lakes periodically by airplane. Air-stocked fingerlings may be of the rainbow, Kamloops rainbow, brook, or brown trout variety. Goldens, Lahontan cutthroats, and other varieties of rainbows have been stocked in the past as well.

Given the limited range of the fly rod, a float tube or canoe can be very helpful when fishing the small lakes in the area. Fly-fishing strategy in these lakes should revolve around structure. Weedy shore-lines should be your first target if no fish are rising. These weedy areas are heavy in aquatic life and provide large quantities of trout food. Rocky points and drop-offs are also good areas to explore thoroughly. In the deeper lakes the fish will usually be found near the shoreline since there is little food in the depths. Conversely, trout in shallow lakes will often hold in the deepest part of the lake except when actively feeding. If you can't locate any feeding fish don't be afraid to troll a nymph or streamer. Pheasant Tail Nymphs and Beadhead Olive Woolly Buggers trolled slowly account for a good number of fish in these lakes.

Fly selections should be modified slightly for fishing the Lakes Basin. Midges, damselflies, and terrestrials are the major hatches at this elevation. Mayflies and caddisflies come off sporadically as well. Griffith's Gnats in sizes 18 to 22 will cover the abundant midge hatches. Marabou damsels work well throughout the year, as will adult dam-selflies. Ant, grasshopper, and beetle patterns work well as attractor patterns. Parachute mayfly patterns are good in the smaller sizes (16 to 20). Woolly Buggers and shiny streamers such as the Blanton's Flash Tail are also productive. Brook trout especially like the shiny gold streamers.

The Lakes Basin area straddles the divide between the Plumas and Tahoe national forests, and can be reached from Graeagle off of Highway 70 or from Bassetts Station on Highway 49. Upper Jamison Campground and Lakes Basin Campground are the primary places to stay in the northern (Plumas NF) portion, while Snag Lake, Salmon Creek, and Sardine campgrounds can be found in the southern (Tahoe NF) portion. Numerous lodges can also be found in the area.

Overnight camping is allowed at Smith Lake, Grass Lake, Wades Lake, Rock Lake, and Jamison Lake. Due to high amounts of day-use traffic, overnight camping is not allowed at Hidden, Lily, Grassy, Long, Mud, Silver, Cub, Little Bear, Big Bear, and Round lakes. Motorbikes are prohibited on all trails. Contact the Beckwourth Ranger District for more details.

Gold Lake (6407 feet)

Over a mile and a half long and three-quarters of a mile wide, Gold Lake is the largest natural lake in the Plumas National Forest. Gold Lake is perhaps best known for the high winds that often curse the area. These winds usually come up before noon and make the lake a thoroughly miserable place to be in a small boat or float tube. If you can manage to fish the lake before or after the wind comes up or on a calm day (it can happen), you are likely to do very well.

Fly fishing is most productive in the shallows around the shoreline at Gold Lake. Look for grassy banks, submerged weed beds, and rocky structure. The most easily accessible places are on the east end of the lake near the outlet stream and at the boat ramp. A rough jeep trail travels around the southeast shore of the lake to Little Gold Lake and Squaw Lake. I would advise against driving this road, but it can be used to access the other end of the lake by foot.

Trout grow large in Gold Lake thanks to large populations of crayfish and red-sided minnows. Rusty-brown Woolly Buggers work well when stripped along the bottom to imitate the crayfish. The minnows feed heavily along the shorelines, and can be imitated with shiny golden Flash Tail Streamers and small Zonkers. Griffith's Gnats, Parachute Adams', and ant patterns are useful when fish are surface feeding. I have also found that Pheasant Tail Nymphs work well fished under an indicator. Troll a Woolly Bugger on a sink-tip or full-sink line to locate the fish if you can't see any risers.

Long Lake Trail

The easiest way to access Long Lake is by a marked trail starting near the Lakes Basin Campground. This is only a half-hour hike, ideal for an angler carrying a float tube. Long Lake is one of the best lakes in the Lakes Basin. Second in size only to Gold Lake, Long Lake is home to Kamloops rainbows. They grow to good size, often exceeding a foot in length. Troll or cast and retrieve weighted Woolly Buggers on a sink-tip line. Be sure to let the fly sink to a good depth here.

From Long Lake you can hike around the west side of the lake and up to Mt. Elwell at 7818 feet. The Long Lake trail interconnects with the Round Lake Loop. The trail around the northwest side of the lake (not shown on all maps) should not be attempted due to thick brush.

Round Lake Loop

This is one of the most popular trails in the Lakes Basin. This 3.75-mile round trip takes you past five trout-bearing lakes, including Round Lake, Silver Lake, Big Bear, Little Bear, and Cub Lake. You can start on this trail from Gold Lake Lodge or Elwell Lodge, and it is well marked. The Round Lake Loop interconnects with the Long Lake Trail and the Pacific Crest Trail.

The Bear Lakes are the most popular destination on the Round Lake Loop. Big Bear, Little Bear, and Cub lakes are ideal day-hikes for families with young children. They also hold fish! Big Bear, being the largest, holds the best fish. Fish the shallow, weedy areas early and late and troll Woolly Buggers on a sink-tip or full-sink line in the middle of the day. Silver Lake and Round Lake are also good. Goldens were planted in Silver years ago, but smallish brookies and rainbows are the main action. Round Lake is interesting because of Prospect Mine, which consisted of a mine shaft sunk below the lake. There is a nice drop-off that is clearly visible at Round Lake. Working this drop-off from a float tube can be productive.

Jamison Lake Trail

This trail starts at the Jamison Mine site in the Plumas Eureka State Park. The Jamison Mine complex is one of the most intact mining camps in the Sierra Nevada. There are numerous bunkhouse type structures and other artifacts. The Jamison Lake Trail accesses four good fishing lakes. The closest is Grass Lake, ideal for a half-day trip with a hike of 30 to 40 minutes. About 2/3 of the way to Grass Lake there is a sign for Jamison Falls, which you can hear from the trail. The small waterfall makes a great backdrop for a picnic.

Grass Lake is very shallow and rich in aquatic life. Consequently, it has some of the best fish in the area. Beyond Grass Lake you have your choice of Wades, Jamison, and Rock lakes, which are another 45 to 60 minutes along the trail. These are all good fish-bearing lakes, supporting fair-sized brookies and rainbows. From Wades Lake you can hike up to the Pacific Crest Trail. The Jamison Lake Trail also interconnects with the Smith Lake Trail.

Smith Lake Trail

Smith Lake is a good destination for a day or half-day trip. The lake is only 30 to 40 minutes from the trailhead, which can be found along the road to Gray Eagle Lodge. Smith Lake has a good damselfly hatch in July, and I've heard rumors that large brook trout can be caught at that time. Unfortunately, I've never been able to confirm this rumor, but I have caught plenty of feisty little rainbows here on small olive Woolly Buggers.

Be sure to investigate the waterfall on the west side of the lake. At first it may sound like the wind blowing through the trees, but there is an impressive little waterfall hidden behind the trees. The water comes from a smaller lake upstream. This is a very pretty lake, and is one of my favorite destinations in the Lakes Basin.

Frazier Falls Trail

A sign along the paved Gold Lake road will direct you to the trailhead for Frazier Falls. This is another popular family destination. A half-mile trail leads to an overlook of the 100-foot falls. There is a picnic area along the trail. This is not really a place to fish, although Frazier Creek does hold some small rainbows and browns downstream from the falls.

Upper and Lower Salmon Lakes

Upper Salmon Lake has good vehicle access and a nice boat ramp. Salmon Lake Resort is located on the opposite side of the lake, and is only accessible by ferry ride from the boat ramp. Upper Salmon Lake is fairly large and rather deep. It also seems a little warmer than some of the other lakes in the area, so bring a full-sink fly line. Lower Salmon Lake is much different. It is a shallow, weedy lake. It can only be accessed by a short 4WD road which branches off from the paved road to Upper Salmon Lake. Consequently, Lower Salmon Lake gets far less fishing pressure than its neighbor. The rainbows grow to twelve inches and better in this food-rich environment. Midges hatch in abundance and provide the majority of the action. Middle Salmon Lake, in between Upper and Lower Salmon, also holds some rainbows, although they are on the small side. Middle Salmon can be fished effectively from shore since it is a very small lake.

Upper and Lower Sardine Lakes

The southernmost of the lakes in the Lakes Basin Area, Upper and Lower Sardine Lakes provide some of the best fishing in the area. Lower Sardine Lake is stocked with catchable brookies on a regular basis. Although normally crowded with boats from Sardine Lodge, this lake is productive for float-tubers trolling or casting small Woolly Buggers. Use a sink-tip or full-sink line to get down to the fish. Upper Sardine is only accessible by a rough, half-mile 4WD road. This lake can be very productive for the angler willing to carry in a float tube or canoe.

Packer Lake

To reach Packer Lake take the road to Lower Sardine Lake and follow the signs. The road is paved all the way to the lake and on up to Packer Saddle, a popular trailhead for the Pacific Crest Trail. Packer Lake provides excellent action on wild and stocked rainbow trout to fifteen inches. Floating lines work well as the lake is shallow, but you may want to try a sink-tip in the deeper end of the lake. Mayfly and midge hatches are common in the afternoon, and can be imitated with Griffith's Gnats and parachute mayfly patterns. Hoppers and adult damselfly patterns work well also.

Deer Lake (7100 feet)

Deer Lake is another popular fishing lake. This is one of the better fishing lakes in the Lakes Basin. You can hike to Deer Lake from a marked trailhead on the road to Packer Lake, or you can drive in on an Off Highway Vehicle (OHV) trail that parallels the Pacific Crest Trail. This OHV trail begins at Packer Saddle (see Packer Lake, page 103). It is rough but passable to most 4WD vehicles. Deer Lake is rather deep, and I would recommend having a full-sink line on hand in case the fish go deep. I have had my best luck when trolling Pheasant Tail Nymphs on floating or sinking lines. Midge hatches are common.

Goose, Haven, and Snag Lakes

These three roadside lakes can provide some decent action on occasion. They are all shallow lakes, and should be fished with floating lines to avoid tangling with the bottom. There is a small campground at Snag Lake. Goose, Haven, and Snag lakes are populated by a mixed bag of brook and rainbow trout.

Young America Lake (7250 feet)

Named after a nearby mine, Young America Lake is one of the highest and most remote lakes in the Lakes Basin. This lake was well-known in the past for its population of golden trout, the state fish of California. Unfortunately, the goldens have been pushed out by the better-suited brook trout. The small brookies cruise the shoreline of the lake and will eagerly take dry flies and small nymphs. The only way to access the lake is by a short but treacherous cross-country hike. The easiest route into the lake is from Tamarack Lakes, which are accessed via a jeep trail that begins near Packer Lake. Tamarack Lakes are also excellent for smallish brookies. You'll need a Sierra City topo map for this hike.

Other Lakes

Other fish-bearing lakes in the Lakes Basin include Spencer Lakes, Little Deer Lake, Hawley Lake, Grassy Lake, Lily Lake, Little Gold Lake, and Squaw Lake.

Plumas-Eureka State Park

The 5,000-acre Plumas-Eureka State Park was established in 1959 to preserve and restore the remains of the single most prosperous hardrock mine in Plumas County. The most impressive remnant is the beautifully restored Plumas-Eureka Mill, which processed over eight million dollars of gold in the 1800s. Although the area had been mined since 1850, an English company called the Sierra Buttes Mining Company, Ltd. consolidated most of the mines near Eureka Peak in 1872. Eureka Lake was raised by a dam to provide water to the ore-crushing stamp mills. Miles of tramways were built to carry ore from the various mines to the mills. Locals claim that these tramways served as the world's first ski lift. Called snow-shoeing or long-boarding, skiing was a popular winter pastime for the mining community.

The Plumas-Eureka mines were prosperous throughout the 1870s and 1880s, employing as many as 400 workers at times. The Sierra Buttes Mining Company sold the mines as they became less productive in the 1890s. Small-scale mining operations were continued until 1943. The Plumas-Eureka State Park was created in 1959, and has become a popular family destination. The park is most easily reached from Blairsden or Graeagle. The park headquarters is staffed year round and includes an excellent museum. Upper Jamison Campground is very nice, and has over 60 campsites.

Eureka Lake and Jamison Creek offer good fishing. Eureka Lake can be reached from the Johnsville Ski Area and holds good brookies and rainbows. From Eureka Lake you can hike up to Eureka Peak at 7,447 feet via the three-mile Eureka Peak Loop Trail. Jamison Creek flows through the park and is stocked occasionally with catchable rainbows. Jamison Creek is good all the way down to Two Rivers, were it flows into the Middle Fork Feather River. In the lower part of the creek away from obvious road accesses there are some really nice wild fish.

Part Three...

STRATEGIES FOR SUCCESS

Appropriate Equipment

Rods

The best all-around fly rod for the Plumas National Forest (and for trout fishing in general) is a nine-foot five-weight. This is a very versatile rod, and is about the most popular configuration being sold today. A five-weight can handle fairly heavy nymphs as well as very fine dry flies. A nine-foot rod also helps to cast into the wind and makes roll casting easier. Be sure to cast several rods before making your decision, as action varies considerably between different brands and models of fly rods. One manufacturer's five-weight may feel like another's three-weight. Also, be sure to buy a rod with a lifetime warranty.

While the nine-foot five-weight is a very workable compromise, other rods may be better suited to some fishing situations. If you plan to fish only the smallest streams, or mainly spring creeks like Yellow Creek, you would be better suited with a short two- or three-weight rod. If your plans include a lot of lake fishing, a longer rod is desirable no matter what your fishing platform. A nine- or ten-foot rod will help to keep your backcasts off the water and will increase your range considerably. A stiff six- or seven-weight rod is the best choice for making long casts all day long. Success in lake fishing increases with casting range, so get a long rod and learn how to cast well with it.

Reels

Most any fly reel will suffice, but as with anything, you get what you pay for. First and foremost, make sure your reel is appropriately-sized for your fly rod. Although a simple palm-drag reel is adequate, it is a good idea to invest in a reel with a good drag system. The drag system will often mean the difference between catching big fish and losing big fish. Several manufacturers even offer lifetime warranties. If you fish like I do, the lifetime warranty may be a very worthwhile investment.

Fly Lines

Fly lines come in as many varieties as fly rods. A floating line is essential. I like double-taper floating lines because they're easy to roll-cast and can be reversed after one end gets worn out. For my heavier lake-fishing outfit, I have a spool with a weight-forward floating line and a spool set up for a shooting-head system. My shooting-head system includes floating, intermediate, and fast-sinking shooting heads. Shooting heads are relatively short fly lines that are looped at both ends. They are very handy for the float-tuber, since they can be changed quickly without restringing the rod. There are many grades of full-sink lines and shooting heads. An intermediate line is very useful since it will sink just below the surface, preventing wave action from affecting your retrieve. A new group of clear intermediate lines, called "sly lines," are popular due to their low visibility. Faster-sinking lines are useful for dredging the bottom during hot summer days.

Sink-tip lines are also helpful. Sink-tip lines are great for lake fishing, since they will get your fly down into the 5- to 10-foot depth range. An intermediate sinking line will do the same, but the sink-tip offers a little more versatility. Sink-tip lines can be used to fish streamers in streams and to get nymphs down deep. I carry an extra spool with a sink-tip line for my 5-weight rod.

Leaders

Long leaders are not necessary for fly fishing the Plumas National Forest. 7 1/2-foot, 4X tapered leaders are standard, although 9-foot tapered leaders are useful for lake fishing. I often add sections of 5X and 6X tippet when fishing small flies on lakes or over spooky fish, but 4X is usually the rule. I have never encountered fish in the Plumas National Forest that were so finicky as to require a tippet smaller than 6X.

Watercraft

The variety of specialized watercraft available to fly-fishers is expanding along with the rest of the industry. Float tubes are no longer "new," prams and canoes are "cool" again, and u-boats, kickboats, and catarafts are the current craze. As with fly rods, anglers are forced to make some kind of compromise. The float tube is the most versatile, but your decision must be based on the type of water you plan to fish the most.

A pontoon boat or pram is a good choice if you're only going to be fishing roadside lakes. The oars allow you to cruise around the lake at a good clip, which is especially handy on the larger reservoirs like Lake Davis and Frenchman. If you plan on any backcountry lake fishing, the float tube or small u-boat is the only option. There are two main types of float tubes, those with a truck tire tube inside and those with a lightweight bladder. If you plan on fishing large reservoirs mainly, you will want to get one with a truck tire tube. They float higher and are much more durable. If you're a backpacker and weight is a concern, you may want to get one with a lightweight air bladder. Some companies make lightweight tubes designed specifically for backpacking but keep in mind that these tubes aren't as durable. I prefer to pack in a heavy-duty tube. My float tube has backpack straps, so I just put it on over my backpack, which fits in the "hole" of the float tube.

One way to increase your float-tubing success is to carry more than one rod. Most float tubes have a Velcro rod holder across the lap that will easily carry a broken-down fly rod. I almost always carry two rods. One is set up with a shooting-head system, and the other with a floating line. The floating line allows me to fire off a cast to a rising fish even if I'm trolling a sinking line with the other rod. Although it is legal to fish with two rods at once, I don't recommend the practice. One fly-fisher, one float tube, and two rods fished at the same time are a recipe for disaster (trust me, I've tried it). You must purchase a California Two-Rod Stamp to fish with two rods (the stamp applies only to lakes).

Waders

The great variety of fishing opportunities in the Plumas National Forest demands a variety of waders. Neoprene chest-waders are not only necessary for float tubing, but they are essential equipment for fishing the North Fork Feather River below and above Belden Forebay in the spring when water temperatures are low. Neoprenes also come in handy when fishing the Middle Fork Feather River in the spring when the water is high. Aside from those two scenarios, fly-fishers can get by with hip boots for most of the stream-fishing in the Plumas National Forest. Wet wading is also popular in the summer. As temperatures soar into the upper 90s, it is much more comfortable to get into the water than to wear waders. If you are going to wet-wade, buy a pair of lightweight felt-soled wading shoes. Attached algae, or periphyton, makes streambed rocks very slippery. Felt-soled wading shoes can actually mean the difference between life and death. An old pair of tennis shoes will not suffice. Metal-studded wading boots and a wading staff are also helpful for wading the North Fork below Belden Forebay.

Clothing

Daytime temperatures are very comfortable during the summer in the Plumas National Forest but night and early morning can be pretty chilly. Bring many layers of clothing so that you can be comfortable in all situations. Raingear is essential. If you plan on fishing early or late in the season, be sure to bring long underwear and some warm, insulating clothing such as down or the newer synthetic materials. Polartec pants and socks worn under neoprene waders can keep your legs warm even in the coldest lakes and streams. Some thought should also be given to one's clothing during the hot summer months. I hate mosquitoes and sunburns, but I hate mosquito spray and sunscreen even worse, so I wear clothing that will protect my arms and legs from the aforementioned adversaries. An old pair of jeans or slacks will also keep brush from tearing up your legs on cross-country hikes.

Other items that are helpful include polarized sunglasses and a hat. Polarized sunglasses work great, but you need a hat with a decent brim to shade them. The hat is also nice for applying cool water to your head on those hot summer days.

Maps

Before you trek off to the Plumas National Forest be sure to pick up a US Forest Service map of the Plumas National Forest. They can be found at Forest Service locations in Oroville, Quincy, and elsewhere. These are great maps; the only problem is they're so big. If you have one, you know what I'm talking about. The Forest Service maps show everything but topographical information. They are up to date so they show all the roads, even logging roads built within the last five years. The only problem is they're nearly useless for backpacking and hiking. That's where the topo maps come in handy. The topo maps covering the area are mostly all over ten years old—some are much older—but they are indispensable to the hiking angler. They may not show all the roads, but they'll show the contour lines, and with a little practice you'll be able to pinpoint your location quickly. When searching for better ways to get to certain spots I always use the Forest Service and topo maps in combination. I have included all the topographic maps that cover the Plumas National Forest in Appendix A.

Safety

If you plan on hiking into some of the more remote areas in the Plumas National Forest, it would be wise to purchase a good first-aid kit and learn how to use it properly. I carry a bag in the bottom of my backpack that includes waterproof matches, some commercial fire-starters, spare food, a compass, a snake-bite kit, an emergency blanket, a whistle, and a few other odds and ends. Be sure to carry a topo map of your area as well. Another item to include on longer hikes is a water filter. If you've had bad experiences with water filters in the past be sure to check out the newer models. The newest backpacking water filters are very lightweight and don't require a body-builder to pump them.

The two main safety hazards to watch out for in the Plumas National Forest are rattlesnakes and poison oak. There are also bears and mountain lions, but your chances of meeting one of them are comparatively slim. Always be alert for rattlesnakes in rocky areas, especially the canyons of the North and Middle Fork Feather River. Carry a snake-bite kit and know how to use it. Poison oak is common in the lower elevations and in the canyons of the major rivers. Learn how to identify poison oak so you can be sure to avoid it.

Aside from plants and animals, visitors should also be aware of several human-related hazards. During your explorations in the Plumas National Forest you are likely to encounter many interesting things. At the end of many trails into the Middle Fork Feather River I have found many makeshift campsites, most of which had a "recently-abandoned" look to them. You will definitely encounter mining relics, perhaps even old structures. Some of these old relics may even be inhabited, and one would be wise not to accidentally surprise anybody camped out in these spots. Open mine shafts are also common, and needless to say you should avoid them. You may also find mining and Indian artifacts. As much as you may want to take home a piece of the Old West, these artifacts are protected by law, and may not be removed. Leave them for others to see and appreciate.

Another thing to keep in mind are the hunting seasons for the various animals. Check California Department of Fish and Game regulations—exact dates of the seasons can change from year to year. In the fall, when deer and bear hunters are active, I wear a blaze orange vest or hat. It also helps to make noise, which is easy if you're fishing with a friend. When out in the woods, two people are always better than one.

Fly Patterns for the Plumas National Forest

Given all the diverse fly-fishing opportunities in the Plumas National Forest, it's been rather difficult to compile a short list of "essential" patterns. I have narrowed the selection down to four groups: dry flies, nymphs, stillwater flies, and local favorites. The dry-fly selection includes imitative dry flies, although many of them can also be used as attractor patterns. On the other end of the spectrum, the selection of local favorites includes big dry flies that are popular for fishing the smaller streams because they are easy to see, float really well, and are suggestive of many kinds of aquatic insects and terrestrials. The stillwater selection includes essential patterns for fishing local lakes, and the nymph selection includes both imitative and suggestive patterns for nymphing in lakes and streams.

— Dries —

Yellow Humpy	Parachute Adams	Stimulator
Elk Hair Caddis	Griffith's Gnat	Bullethead Parahopper

— Nymphs —

Rubberleg Stone	Hare's Ear	Prince Nymph
Pheasant Tail	Beadhead Bird's Nest	

— Lake Flies —

Simple Damsel	Snail Flies	Rusty Leech
Blood Midge	Woolly Buggers	

— Local Favorites —

Mill Creek Queen (10)	Royal Wulff (10)	Wendell Special (10)
Rio Grande King (10)	Yellow Palmer (8)	

— Other Effective Patterns —

Dave's Hopper (6-10)	Muddler Minnow (4-10)	Brown Bivisible (12)
Schroeder's Para-Hopper (6-10)	Olive Matuka (6)	Milt's Pond Smelt (2)
Takahashi Damsel (12)	Ascending Midge Pupa (18)	Milt's *Hexagenia* Para-dun (6)
Burk's Bug-eye Damsel (12)	Brassie (18)	Milt's *Hexagenia* Nymph (6)
Barr's Damsel (12)	Sheep Creek Special (10-14)	*Hexagenia* Emerger (12)
No-Name Damsel (12)	Mathews' Sparkle Dun (14-18)	*Hexagenia* Cripple (6)
Trico Spinner (18-22)	Black Ant (8-14)	Blanton's Flash Tail (8-12)
Fall River Special (12-16)	Glo Bug (10)	Zonker (2-6)
		Carcass Patterns (2-6)

Nymphs and Nymphing

There are several nymphing techniques that will help you to connect with subsurface-feeding fish in the Plumas National Forest. The first, and easiest, is indicator nymphing. This technique works very well for fishing long runs. A good indicator nymph setup starts with the leader. The "drop," or the distance between the indicator and nymph, should be one-and-a-half times the depth of water to be fished. There should only be tippet in between the indicator and the nymph. For example, if the water is six feet deep and the trout demand a 5X tippet, you should have nine feet of 5X tippet below your indicator. There is no point in having any line below the indicator that is thicker than the tippet, because the larger diameter line causes more drag through the water, and will pull your fly up and away from the bottom. The smaller diameter line will straighten out more once in the water and will telegraph strikes much better. One or more split shot may be necessary to sink your fly to the bottom, and they should be attached about five to ten inches above the fly. Set the hook on any unnatural movement of the strike indicator.

When fishing pocket water, there really isn't enough room to use the indicator-nymph setup. In this situation short-line nymphing works best. Position yourself directly across from the pocket you want to fish, about a rod's length away. Cast directly upstream and lead the nymph downstream with the rod tip, maintaining just enough tension to see the strike. Watch the end of your fly line. Set the hook whenever you see the slightest hesitation or pull on the line. If you feel the strike you're too late. Since you need to get up close for this technique to work, it is best suited to less-than-clear streams and to whitewater pockets where the fish aren't as likely to see you. This is a deadly technique on the North Fork below Belden Forebay.

The third nymphing technique comes in handy when fishing deep pools on the larger streams. Oftentimes I have found myself standing on a rock just below the head of a giant plunge pool, watching trout feeding at the very limit of my vision. In this situation, take off the indicator and lengthen your leader considerably, maybe as much as twelve or fifteen feet. Attach several large split shot, and swing your fly into the current upstream. I say "swing" because it's not really possible to cast this rig. Hold the rod out above the water, following the line as it travels with the current. The line between the rod tip and the water serves as your strike indicator. A few small clumps of indicator putty at two foot intervals along the leader can make it easier to detect strikes. The takes can be very soft, but occasionally a fish will impale itself on the fly and you'll be able to see or feel the strike. This is a very difficult technique but it can be a real savior on summer days when the fish are down deep.

Some of my favorite searching nymph patterns include the Pheasant Tail Nymph, Bird's Nest, Hare's Ear, and Prince Nymph. I have included the Beadhead Bird's Nest as an example of a beadhead pattern. Each of the patterns listed can be tied with a bead head. Beadhead flies have become very popular because they sink well and have a sparkle that attracts trout. I am also fond of nymphs tied with bead-chain eyes. The bead-chain eyes add weight and give the fly a real bug-eyed look. They also make the fly swim "upside-down," resulting in less snags.

Fishing Through the Seasons

Seasonal changes dictate changes in fishing tactics. This is particularly true at high elevations, where the seasonal changes can be rather drastic. There are four distinct seasons in the Plumas National Forest, and the angler must change tactics frequently to stay on top of the fish.

Spring

The months of April, May, and June see warming temperatures that melt the majority of the snowpack in the Plumas National Forest. The last Saturday in April also happens to be Opening Day of the general trout season in the mountain streams. Since the streams are so high in the spring it is a good idea to focus your efforts on tailwaters. The North Fork Feather River below Belden Forebay, Indian Creek below Antelope Lake, and Little Last Chance Creek below Frenchman Reservoir are popular early-season destinations. The free-flowing streams are usually blown out and entirely unfishable through the middle of May, depending upon the amount of snowfall. By mid-June most streams should be in pretty decent shape for fly fishing.

The reservoirs ice-out between March and May. With a few exceptions, the lakes in the Plumas National Forest are open to fishing year round. The areas near tributary inlets can be very good in the spring, as large amounts of runoff wash all sorts of goodies into the lake. Fishing from shore can be difficult this time of year, as the reservoirs are usually full or nearly full, and there are often trees right up to the water's edge. A decent roll cast can often reach the fish, but you might try fishing from an anchored boat or float tube. Large nymphs fished on a sinking line or deep under an indicator work well in the inlets. Fish are also active along the shoreline in the spring.

Summer

By July the fishing is pretty much wide open all over the Plumas National Forest. The damselfly hatch is on at Lake Davis and Frenchman Lake, the hex hatch is on at Butt Valley Reservoir, the streams are in prime fly-fishing condition, and the high-country lakes are accessible and fishing well. The inlet areas of the reservoirs are also still highly productive.

By August the surface temperatures of the reservoirs rise into the uncomfortable range for trout, and shore fishing is productive only in the early morning and late evening. Sink-tip or full-sink fly lines can help you reach the fish. As the reservoirs become less productive, consider hiking in to some of the backcountry areas of the Plumas National Forest. August is a great time to fish the high lakes in the Lakes Basin. The Middle Fork Feather River is also excellent, as are many of the smaller streams in the area. Some of the best hike-in creeks are Willow Creek, the Little North Fork, Grizzly Creek, Yellow Creek, and Bear Creek. Hopper patterns work very well this time of year. Lower Bucks Lake and Grizzly Forebay fish well this time of year because of their cooler water temperatures.

Fall

This is the favorite season for the locals. Not only is this the most beautiful time of year, but the kids are back in school and the campgrounds are nearly empty (many of them are closed, unfortunately). The tourists are gone for the most part, and the fishing is excellent.

As soon as reservoir surface temperatures drop into a comfortable range, the trout will begin feeding on the surface. This usually happens sometime between Labor Day and the first of October. By this time lake levels are low enough that you can easily fish from the shore. Fall fly fishing can be a lot of fun on the reservoirs in the Plumas National Forest. Fish cruise the shallows, rising in patterns. Some fish rise as they cruise. As soon as you see what direction they're going you can land a cast right in front of the fish. I have also seen fish that will rise periodically in the same spot. You can actually time their rises. You don't need a stop-watch or anything, but if you watch the fish for a little while you'll have an idea of when it will rise again, and that's the time to cast to the fish. I have found that the fish aren't overly selective in the fall. If you put your fly right in front of their nose they will most often take it.

The stream angler must also change tactics in the fall. With cooling water temperatures the trout become less active. The warm afternoon hours are usually the best time of day to fish. The trout move from the heads of the pools to the tailouts, where they don't have to contend with as much current. As the afternoon sun warms the water the fish may start to rise to midges, and become vulnerable to the angler. Large browns may also chase streamers in the larger streams this time of year. Most of the browns spawn before the end of the season on November 15.

Winter

You can usually drive into the larger reservoirs well into November, and sometimes even in December, depending on the weather. Big fish cruise the shorelines right up until the lakes ice over. You can do very well from shore, as big fish often move into very shallow water in search of aquatic snails and other morsels. If you plan on float-tubing this time of year come prepared with appropriate clothing. Fishing gloves, Polartec pants, and warm socks can be a big help. Lakes Davis and Frenchman are good early winter producers, but the reservoirs aren't the only game in town, so to speak.

It's a little-known fact that miles and miles of the forks of the Feather River are open year round. Fortunately for the angler suffering from cabin fever, portions of these rivers are in Butte County, which is part of the Valley District. Streams in the Valley District are open year round. I don't think that a lot of people know about this, since I get a lot of weird looks from passing motorists when I'm strapping on my waders and stringing up my rod in the middle of winter. The North Fork Feather River is easily accessible along Highway 70 in the winter. Milsap Bar on the Middle Fork Feather River is also in Butte County.

Conclusion

The Plumas National Forest offers many opportunities for the fly-fisher, and I have done my best to illustrate each and every one. The most outstanding waters in my opinion are the Middle Fork of the Feather River, the North Fork Feather River at Caribou, Lake Davis, Butt Valley Reservoir, Frenchman Lake, and Yellow Creek. However, you would be missing out if you didn't pay some attention to the lesser-known streams and lakes. Visiting the more remote fishing spots will allow you to see more of the majestic scenery that is characteristic of the Plumas National Forest. You might just catch some nice fish, too!

There is a growing trend amongst Californians to travel elsewhere to enjoy the fine sport of fly fishing. I've had numerous anglers tell me, "Frankly, I just don't get too excited about fly fishing in California anymore." I love to travel and fish in new places, but you don't have to go to Montana for excellent fly fishing. It's right here in California, and there would be a lot more of it if we pushed for tighter angling restrictions, restored more trout habitat, and utilized our hatcheries more constructively. Groups like CalTrout, Trout Unlimited, and the Federation of Fly-fishers are pushing for these reforms in California, but these organizations must be supported by dedicated people. We must write letters, volunteer our labor, and yes, even donate money, if we wish for serious progress in California's trout fisheries.

Please practice conservation when fishing in the Plumas National Forest, or anywhere else for that matter. Release the majority of your catch. Pack out what you pack in. Pick up litter left behind by others. Check out conservation groups to see what you can do to improve the streams and lakes where you like to fish. Perhaps most importantly, remember to take your eyes off the water every once in a while and enjoy the scenery. It's a beautiful world out there, and if you're too intent on your fishing, you might just miss It!

Bibliography/Further Reading

California Trout. *Yellow Creek: For California, A Rare Spring Creek Angling Experience.*

Cutter, Ralph. *Sierra Trout Guide.* Frank Amato Publications. Portland, Oregon. 1991.

Department of Parks and Recreation. *Plumas-Eureka State Park.* The Resources Agency, State of California. 1978.

Department of Water Resources. *California's State Water Project.* State of California. 1988.

Fariss & Smith. *Illustrated History of Plumas, Lassen & Sierra Counties.* San Francisco, California. 1882.

Forest Service. "A Guide to the Bucks Lake Wilderness" (Forest Service map). United States Department of Agriculture. 1991.

Forest Service. "Hiking Trails-Lakes Basin (Beckwourth District)," United States Department of Agriculture.

Forest Service. "Plumas National Forest" (Forest Service map). United States Department of Agriculture. 1992.

Hafele, Rick and Dave Hughes. *The Complete Book of Western Hatches.* Frank Amato Publications. Portland, Oregon. 1981.

Hanley, Ken. *California Fly Tying and Fishing Guide.* Frank Amato Publications. Portland, Oregon. 1991.

Martin, Jim. *Guidebook to the Feather River Country.* Ward Ritchie Press. Los Angeles, California. 1972.

Plumas County Visitors Bureau. *Plumas County Visitors Guide.* Feather Publishing Co., Inc. Quincy, California. 1996.

Whitlock, Dave. *Guide to Aquatic Trout Foods.* Lyons & Burford. New York, New York. 1982.

Available from the Plumas County Museum

Barrett, L. A.. *Early Day History of Lassen and Plumas Forests.*

Hutchison, W. H. *Tales of Pioneer Plumas.* Plumas County Fair. 1954.

James, III, Charles D. *The Naming of the Feather River.*

Lawson, Scott. *Early Gold Mining in Plumas County.* The Plumas County Historical Society. Publication Number 56. 1991.

Martin, James. "Ghost Towns Are Not Always Old Timers: Walker Mine." The *Sacramento Bee.* Sept. 17, 1961.

Valey, Nicholas N. *History of the Feather River Canyon Power.* Storrie, California.

KAREN HARRIS BOONE

A third generation native of Northern California, Andrew has visited the Plumas National Forest every summer since he was born. It was there that he gained an appreciation for the outdoors while he taught himself how to fly fish. Andrew's familiarity with the area grew rapidly during his high school and early college years where he spent four summers working at Bucks Lake Lodge. When he wasn't working, Andrew explored the lakes and streams of the surrounding Plumas National Forest. Andrew recently graduated from the University of California at Davis with a degree in Environmental and Resource Science. He has spent the last two summers guiding for Clearwater House on Hat Creek in Cassel, California. Andrew is dedicated to the conservation of California's natural resources and is looking forward to a career in environmental law.

APPENDIX A: TOPOGRAPHICAL MAP COVERAGE OF THE PLUMAS NATIONAL FOREST

The following 7.5-minute topographical maps may be helpful when fishing the Plumas National Forest. They can be bought locally or ordered from the U.S. Geological Survey at the following address:

U.S. Geological Survey
Box 25286 Denver Federal Center
Denver, CO 80225

Be sure to request an index and a catalog of published maps. You may also want to request a key to the topographical map symbols.

Almanor: Lake Almanor, Butt Valley Reservoir, Butt Creek
American House: S. F. Feather River, Little Grass Valley Res., Fall River
Antelope Lake: Antelope Lake, Indian Creek
Babcock Peak
Belden: North Fork Feather River, Chips Creek
Berry Creek: North Fork Feather River
Blairsden: Middle Fork Feather River
Blue Nose Mountain: Middle Fork Feather River, Nelson Creek
Brush Creek: Middle Fork Feather River, Little North Fork
Bucks Lake: Bucks Lake, Lower Bucks Lake
Canyondam: North Fork Feather River, Lake Almanor
Caribou: North Fork, East Branch N. F., Belden Forebay, Butt Lake
Cascade: Middle Fork Feather River, South Branch Middle Fork
Chilcoot: Little Last Chance Creek
Clio
Clipper Mills: South Fork Feather River, Lost Creek, Lost Creek Reservoir
Crescent Mills: Indian Creek, East Branch North Fork, Spanish Creek
Crocker Mountain: Lake Davis
Diamond Mountain

Dixie Mountain
Dogwood Peak: Middle Fork Feather River, Bear Creek
Ferris Creek: Last Chance Creek
Forbestown: South Fork Feather River
Frenchman Lake: Frenchman Lake, Little Last Chance Creek
Genesee Valley: Indian Creek
Gold Lake: Lakes Basin
Goodyears Bar: Canyon Creek
Greenville
Grizzly Valley: Lake Davis
Haskins Valley: Middle Fork Feather River, Willow Creek
Johnsville: Middle Fork Feather River
Kettle Rock: Taylor Lake
La Porte: Little Grass Valley Reservoir, Slate Creek, Canyon Creek
Meadow Valley: Spanish Creek
Moonlight Peak
Mt. Fillmore: Canyon Creek
Mt. Ingalls: Little Grizzly Creek
Onion Valley: Middle Fork Feather River, Onion Valley Creek
Portola: Middle Fork Feather River, Big Grizzly Creek
Pulga: North Fork Feather River
Quincy: Spanish Creek
Sierra City: Lakes Basin
Soapstone Hill: Grizzly Creek, Little North Fork
Spring Garden
Squaw Valley Peak
Stony Ridge
Storrie: North Fork Feather River, Bucks Creek, Grizzly Forebay
Strawberry Valley: Sly Creek Reservoir, North Yuba River, Canyon Creek
Taylorsville: Indian Creek
Twain: North Fork, East Branch North Fork

APPENDIX B: SOURCES OF INFORMATION

Plumas National Forest Supervisor's Office
159 Lawrence Street
Box 11500
Quincy, CA 95971
(530) 283-2050

Oroville Ranger District: (530) 534-6500
La Porte Ranger District: (530) 675-2462
Quincy Ranger District: (530) 283-0555
Beckwourth Ranger District: (530) 836-2575
Greenville Ranger District: (530) 284-7126
Milford Ranger District: (530) 253-2223

Plumas County Visitors Bureau
91 Church St., P.O. Box 4120
Quincy, CA 95971
(800) 326-2247

Plumas-Eureka State Park
Johnsville Star Route
Blairsden, California 96103
(530) 836-2380

California Department of Fish and Game, Region 2
1701 Nimbus Road
Rancho Cordova, CA 95670
(916) 358-2900
Fish Plant Recording: (916) 351-0832

California Trout
870 Market St., #857
San Francisco, CA 94102

Plumas County Museum
500 Jackson Street
Quincy, CA 95971
(530) 283-6320

Appendix C: Tables

FISHING DESTINATION	TYPES OF FISH	ACCESS
Antelope Lake	Rainbow trout, brown trout	Paved road
Bucks Lake/Lower Bucks Lake	Rainbow trout, brown trout, brook trout, kokanee, mackinaw	Paved road, dirt road
Butt Valley Reservoir	Rainbow trout, brown trout	Dirt road
Frenchman Lake	Rainbow trout, brown trout	Paved road
Gold Lake/Lakes Basin Area	Rainbow trout, brown trout, brook trout, mackinaw	Paved road, dirt road, trail
Lake Davis	Rainbow trout, brown trout	Paved road dirt road
Little Grass Valley Reservoir	Rainbow trout, brown trout kokanee	Paved road
Middle Fork Feather River	Rainbow trout, brown trout	Trail, Dirt road
North Fork Feather River	Rainbow trout, brown trout	Paved road
Yellow Creel	Rainbow trout, brown trout	Dirt road

CAMPGROUNDS	NEAREST LODGING*	BEST SEASON
Boulder Creek, Lone Rock, Long Point; 188 sites	Quincy, 50 miles Westwood, 40 miles	May-July, Oct.-Nov.
Haskins Valley, Sundew, Whitehorse, Mill Creek, Lower Bucks, Grizzly Creek; 127 sites	Bucks Lake Lodge Bucks Lakeshore Resort	May-July, Sep.-Nov.
Ponderosa Flat, Cool Springs; 93 sites	Lake Almanor, Chester, 10 miles	July-Oct.
Big Cove, Chilcoot, Cottonwood Springs, Frenchman, Spring Creek; 171 sites	Portola, 25 miles Reno, 40 miles	Apr.-July, Oct.-Dec.
Lakes Basin, Upper Jamison; 90 sites	Various lodges	June-Sep.
Grasshopper Flat, Grizzly, Lightning Tree; 181 sites	Portola, 7 miles Reno, 50 miles	Apr.-July, Oct.-Dec.
Black Rock, Little Beaver, Peninsula, Red Feather, Running Deer; 250 sites	La Porte, 5 miles	May-July, Sep.-Nov.
Cleghorn Bar, Milsap Bar; 12 sites	Quincy, 10 miles La Porte, 15 miles	June-Nov.
Gansner Bar, Hallsted, North Fork, Queen Lily; 66 sites	Belden, Paxton, Twain, Tobin, Oroville, 30 miles	May-July, Sept.-Nov.
Yellow Creek; 10 sites	Belden, 15 miles Chester, 15 miles	May-July, Sept.- Nov.

* contact the Plumas County Visitors Bureau for more details

APPENDIX D: FLY SHOPS AND GUIDES

Allan Bruzza's Sportsman's Den
1580 East Main St.
Quincy, CA 95971
(530) 283-2733

Bob's Fly Shack
488 W. Onstott Road
Yuba City, CA 95991
(530) 671-9628

Chico Fly Shop
932 W. 8th Ave., Ste. D
Chico, CA 95926
(530) 345-9983

Grizzly Country Store (Lake Davis)
7552 Lake Davis Rd.
Portola, CA 96122
(530) 832-0270

Milt Jensen's
Merganser Outfitters
P.O. Box 45
Chico, CA 95927
(530) 343-4071

Reno Fly Shop
249 East Moana Lane, #14
Reno, NV 89502
(702) 825-3474

INDEX

Treat yourself
and your angling partner . . .

...to a fly fishing and tying feast with subscriptions to *Flyfishing & Tying Journal.* You'll marvel at the helpful, colorful creativity inside this 100-plus page quarterly masterpiece of publishing! You've worked hard, now sit back and drink in the elixir of fly-fishing potential that we provide you, featuring fine printing on top-quality paper. We are terribly excited with our generous, friendly fly-fishing publication and know you will love it also! Please share our joy of discovery and subscribe today!

Strike a deal
for only $9.99 for one year.

Order a subscription below for you and your angling friend.

- -

SUBSCRIBE HERE!

Please send me:

☐ One year of *Flyfishing & Tying Journal* for only $9.99 (4 big issues)

☐ Two years of *Flyfishing & Tying Journal* for only $19.95 (8 issues)

☐ Check enclosed (US Funds)   ☐ New ☐ Renew

☐ Charge to:

☐ Visa ☐ MC CC#:_____ Exp: _____

(Canadian & foreign orders please add $5/year)

Phone orders: 1-800-541-9498 or 503-653-8108. FAX 503-653-2766.
Call 8 to 5 M-F, Pacific Standard Time.

Name:_____

Day Phone:(_____) _____

Address: _____

City:_____ State:_____ Zip: _____

FRANK AMATO PUBLICATIONS • P.O. BOX 82112 • PORTLAND, OR 97282